WOW BODS

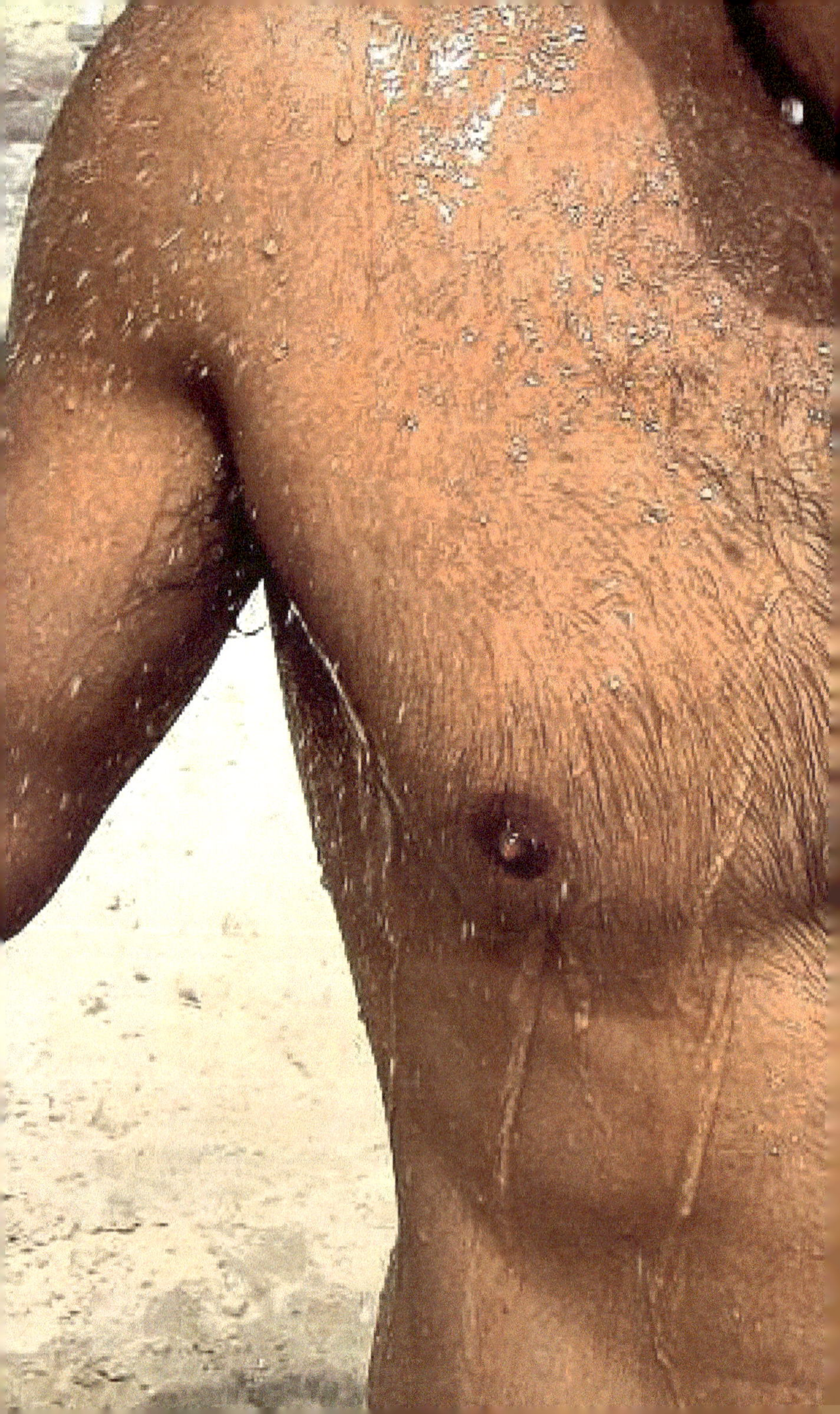

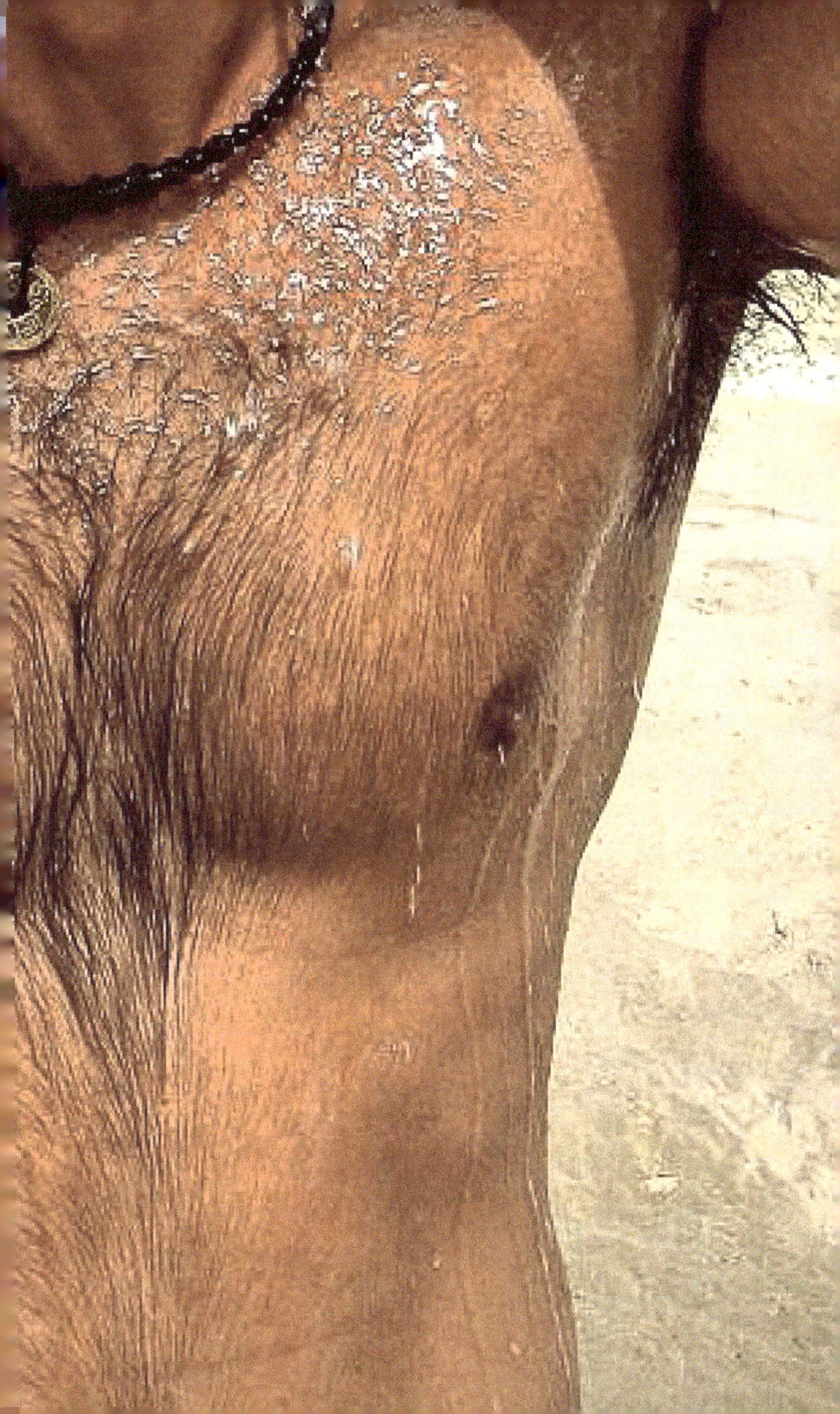

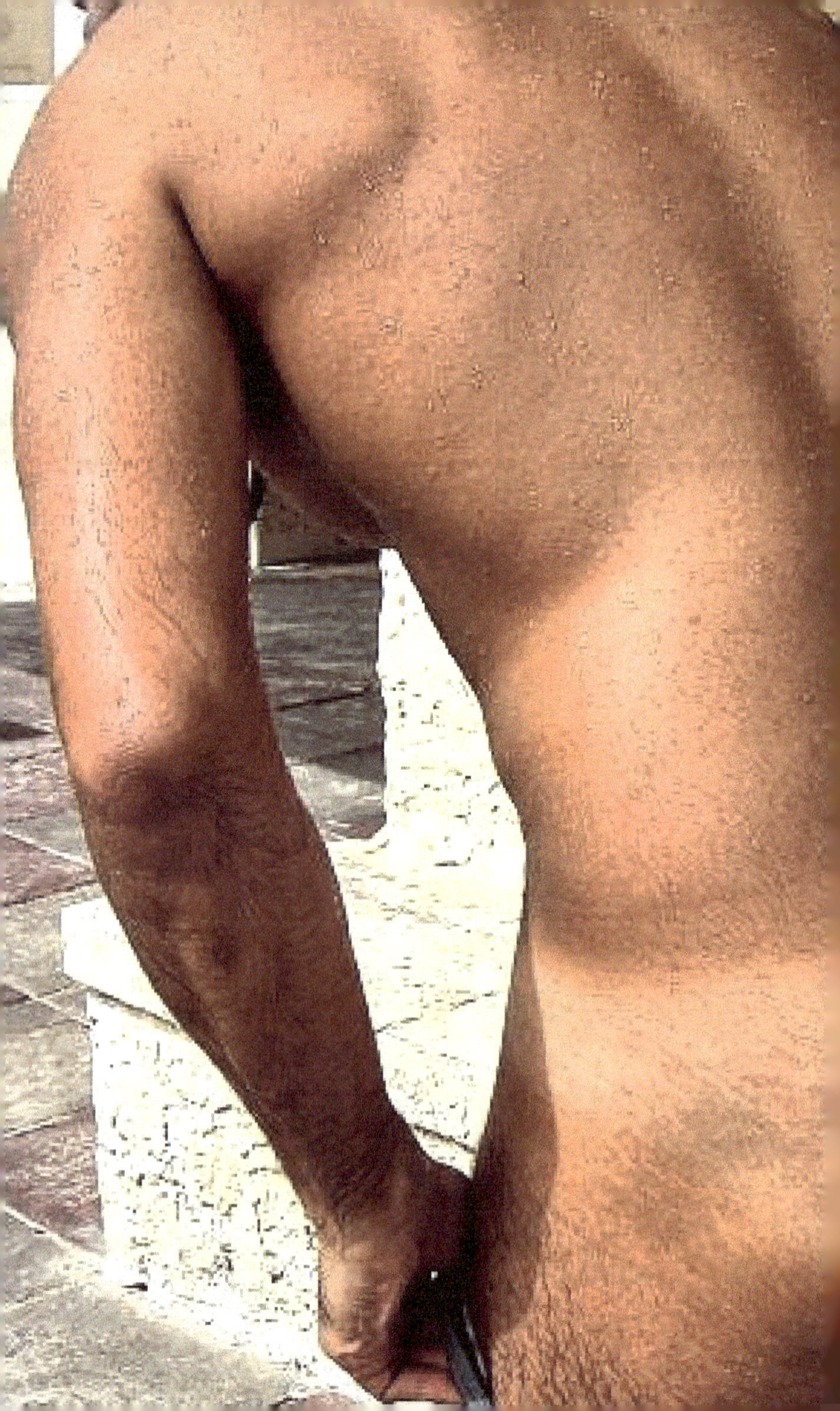

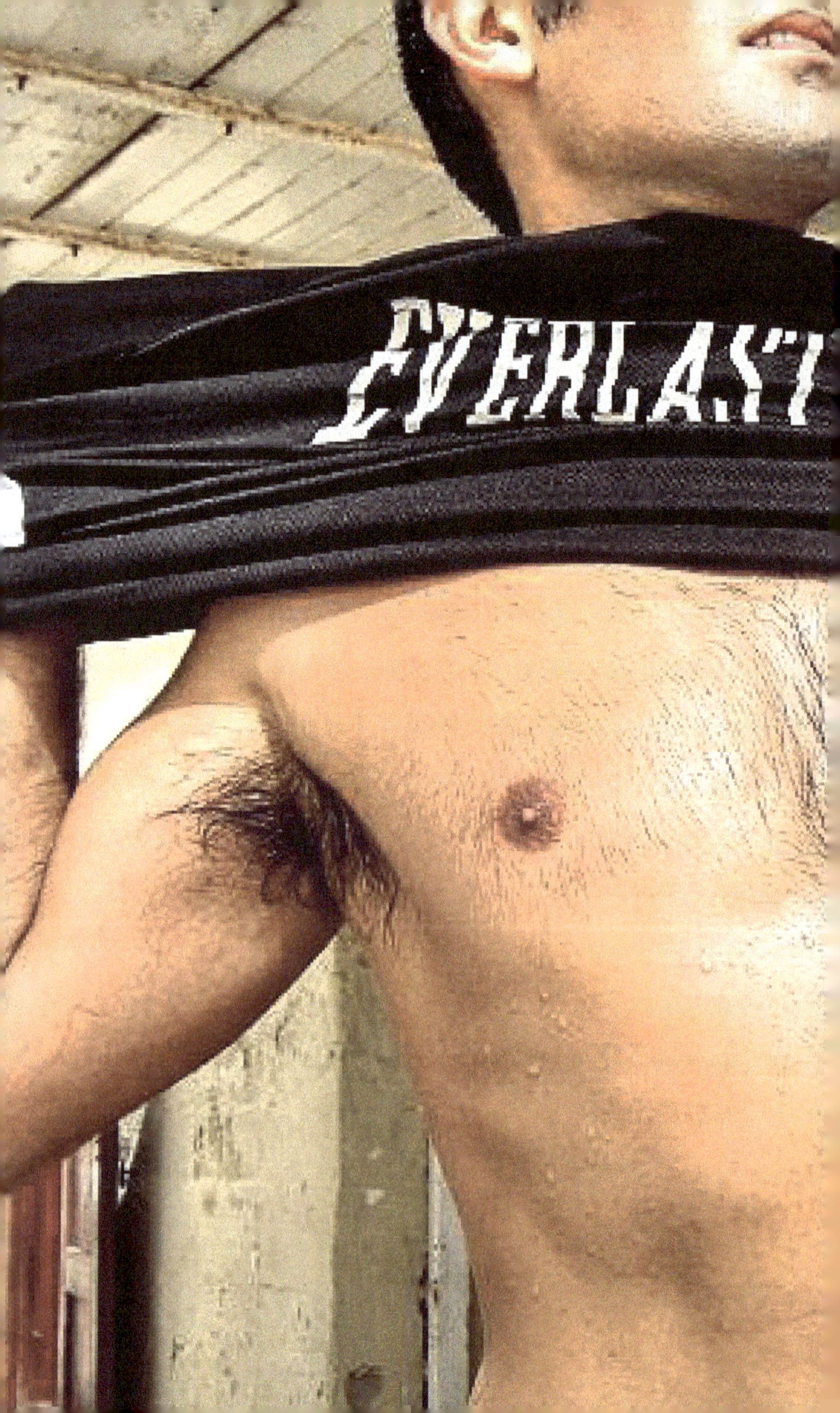
EVERLAST

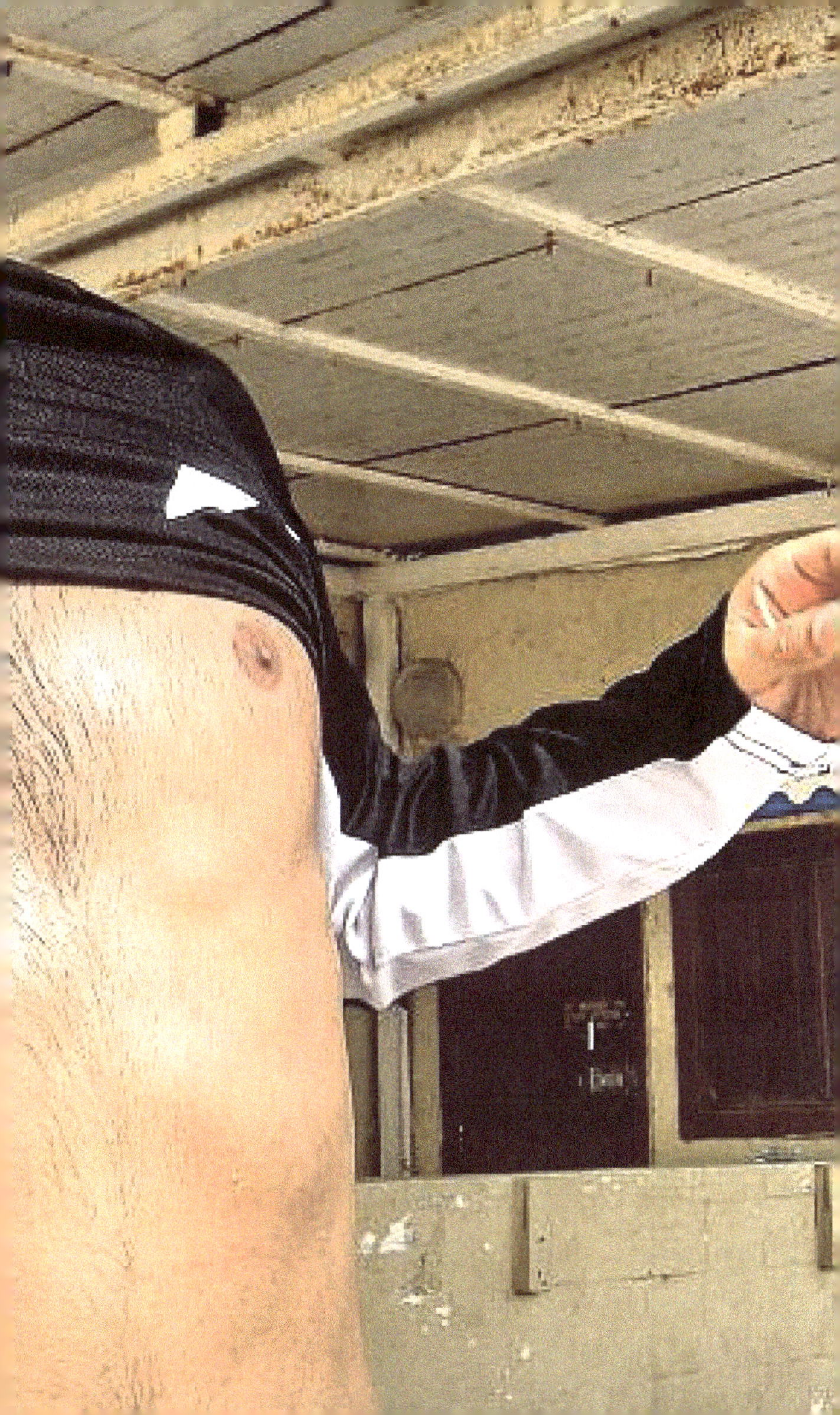

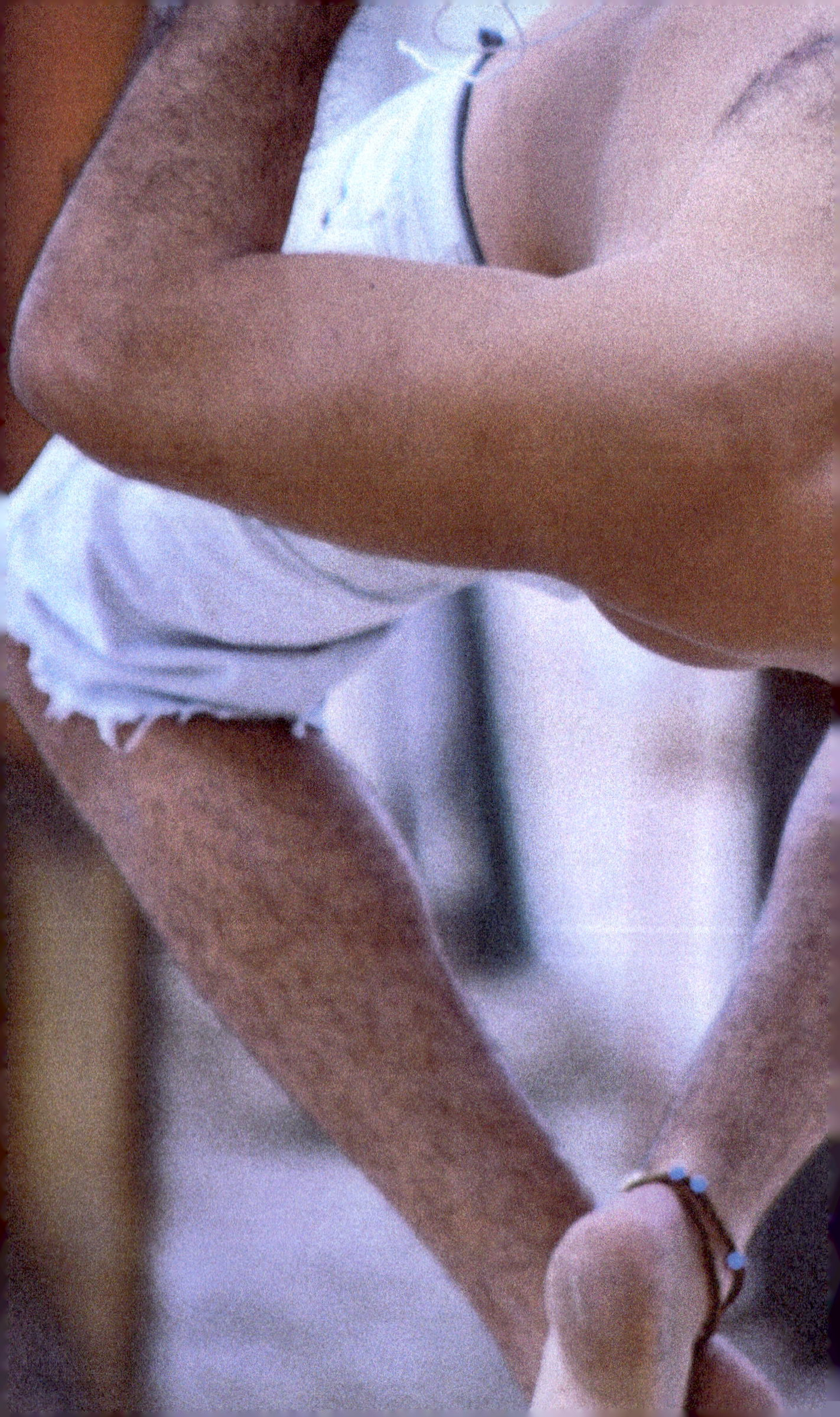

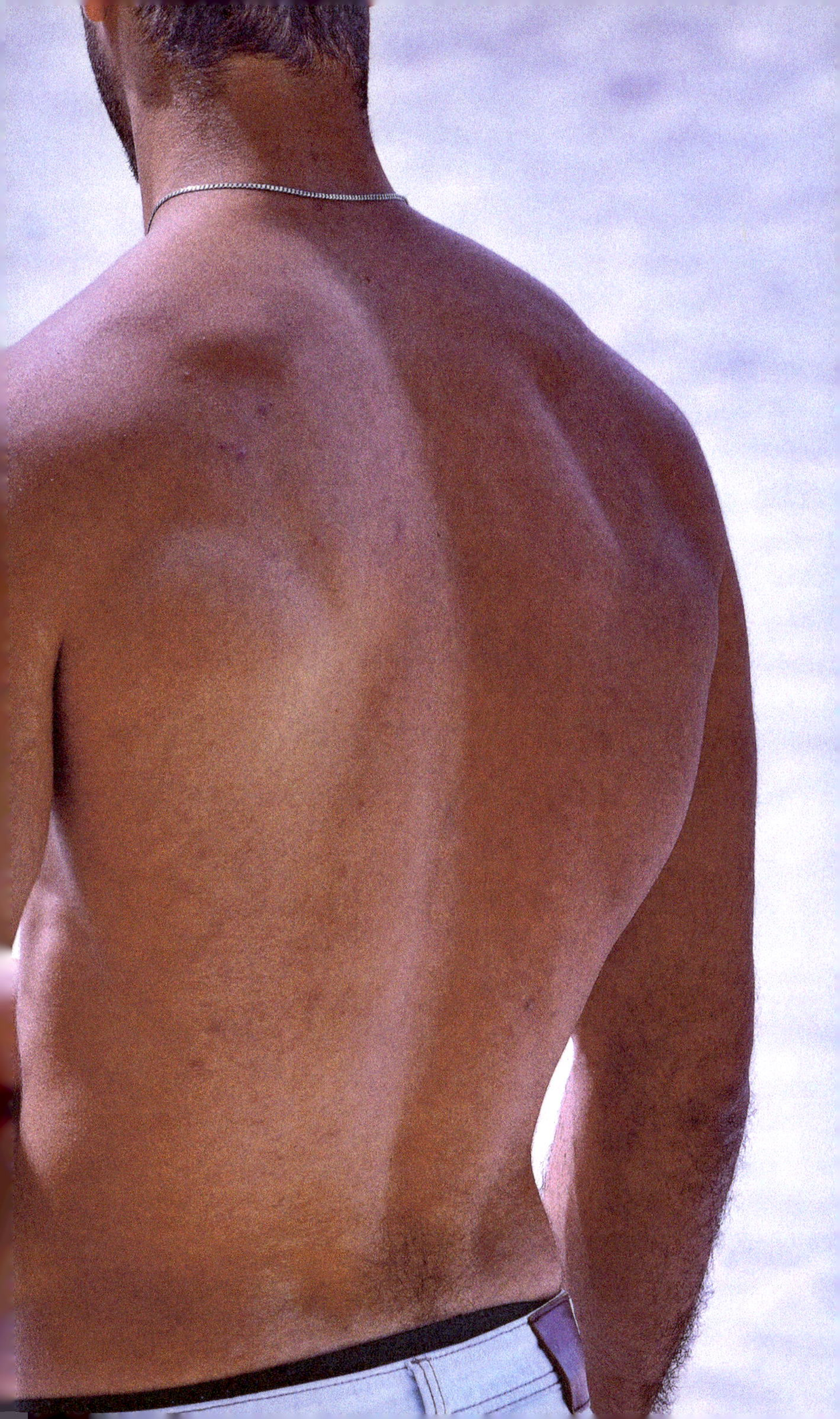

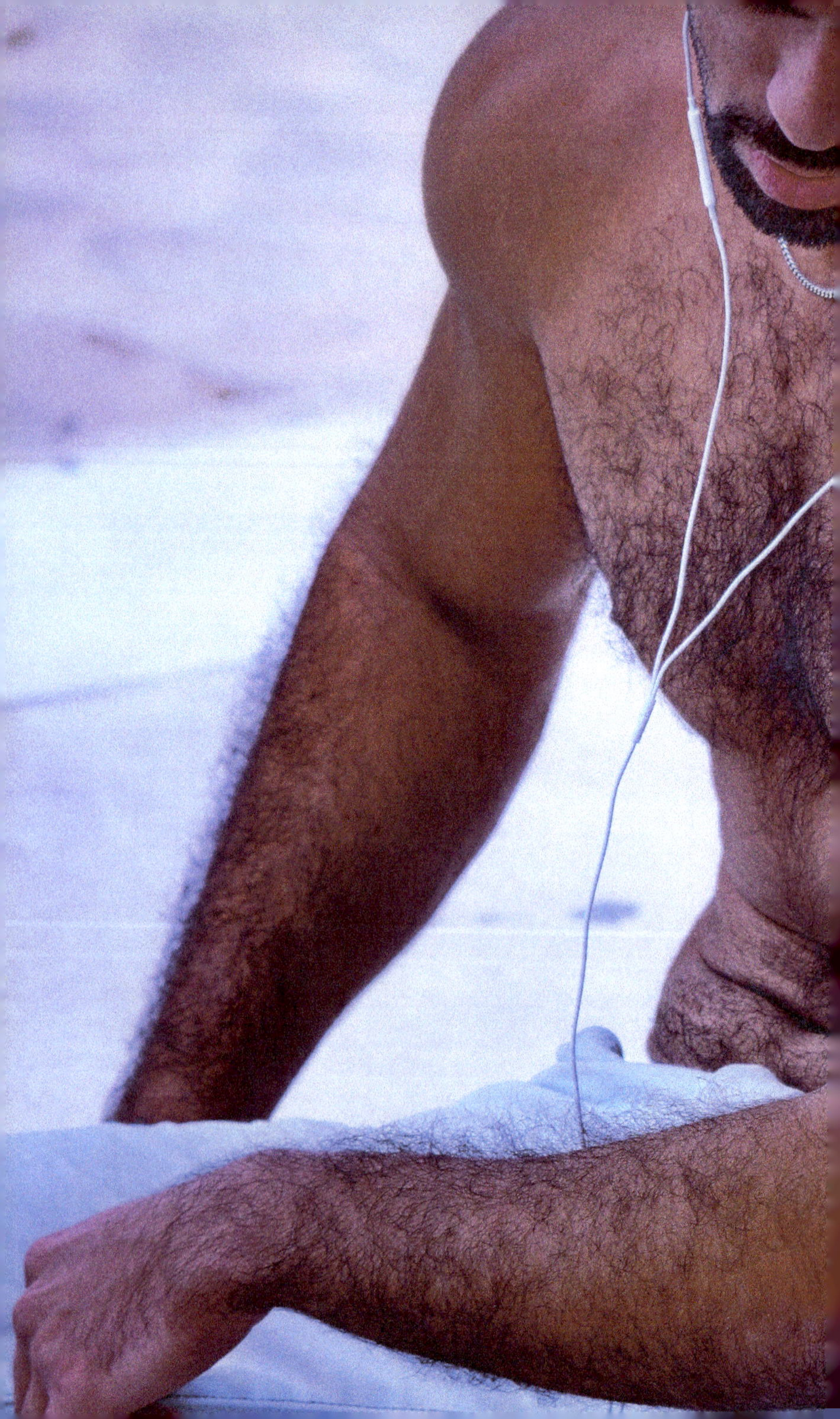

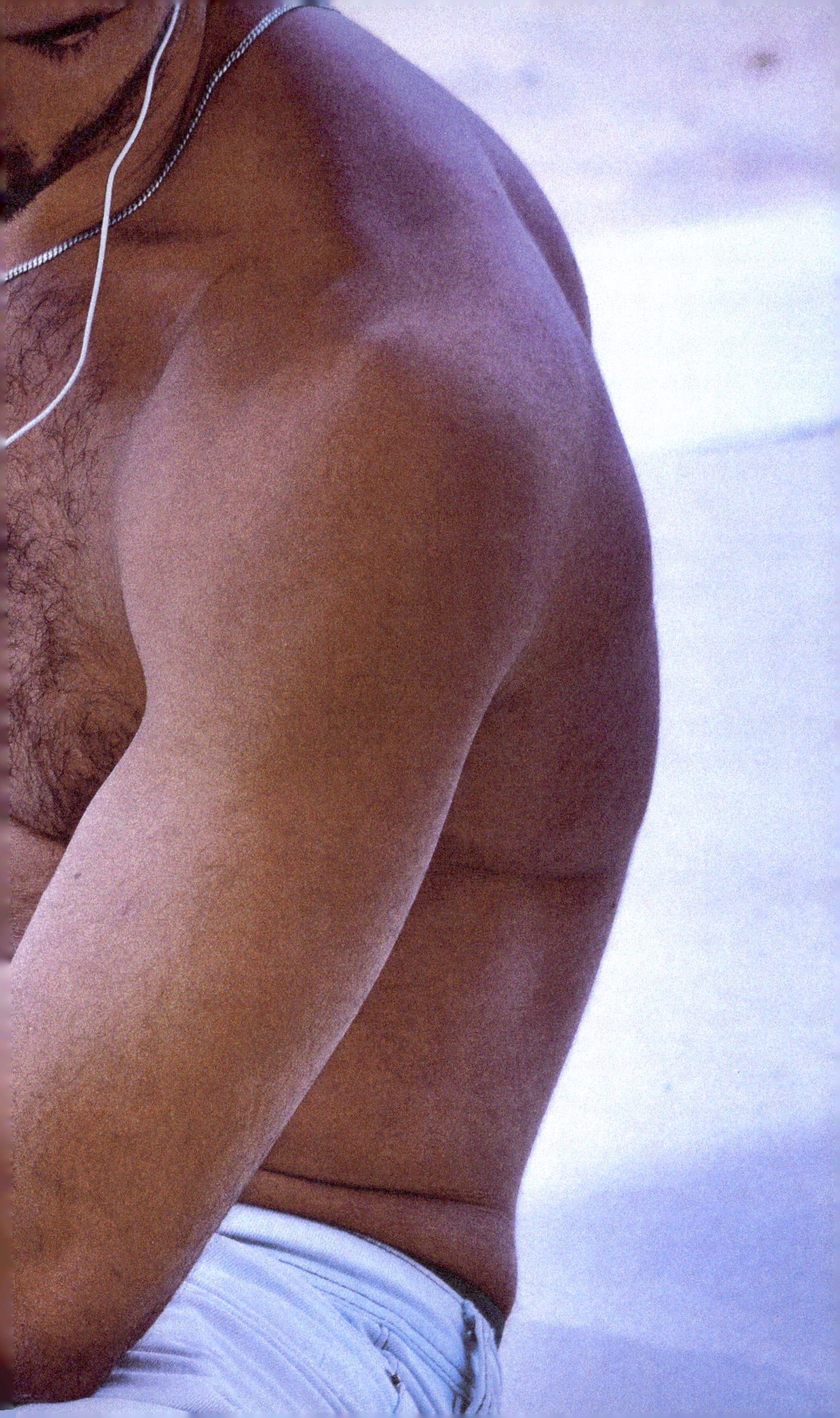

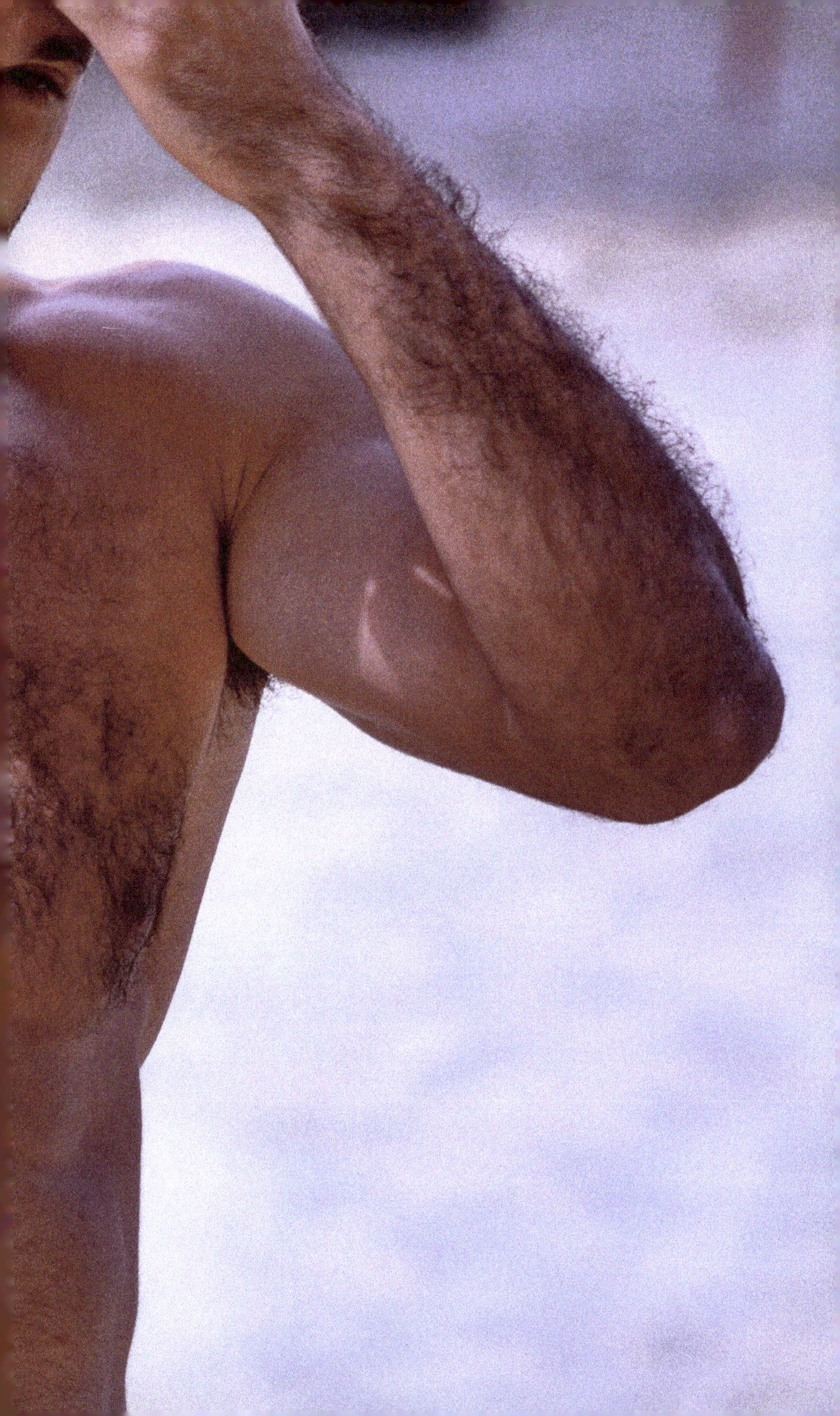

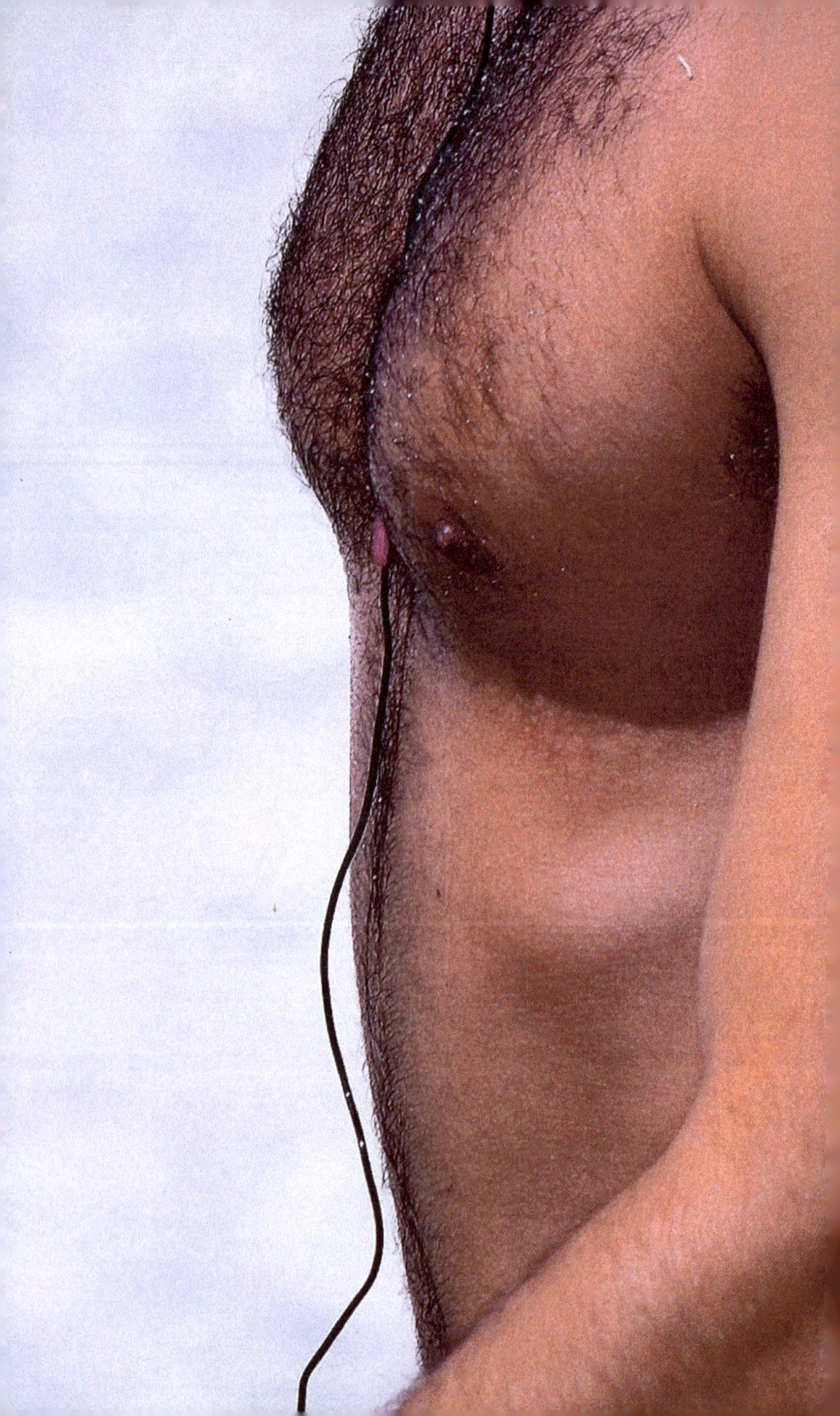

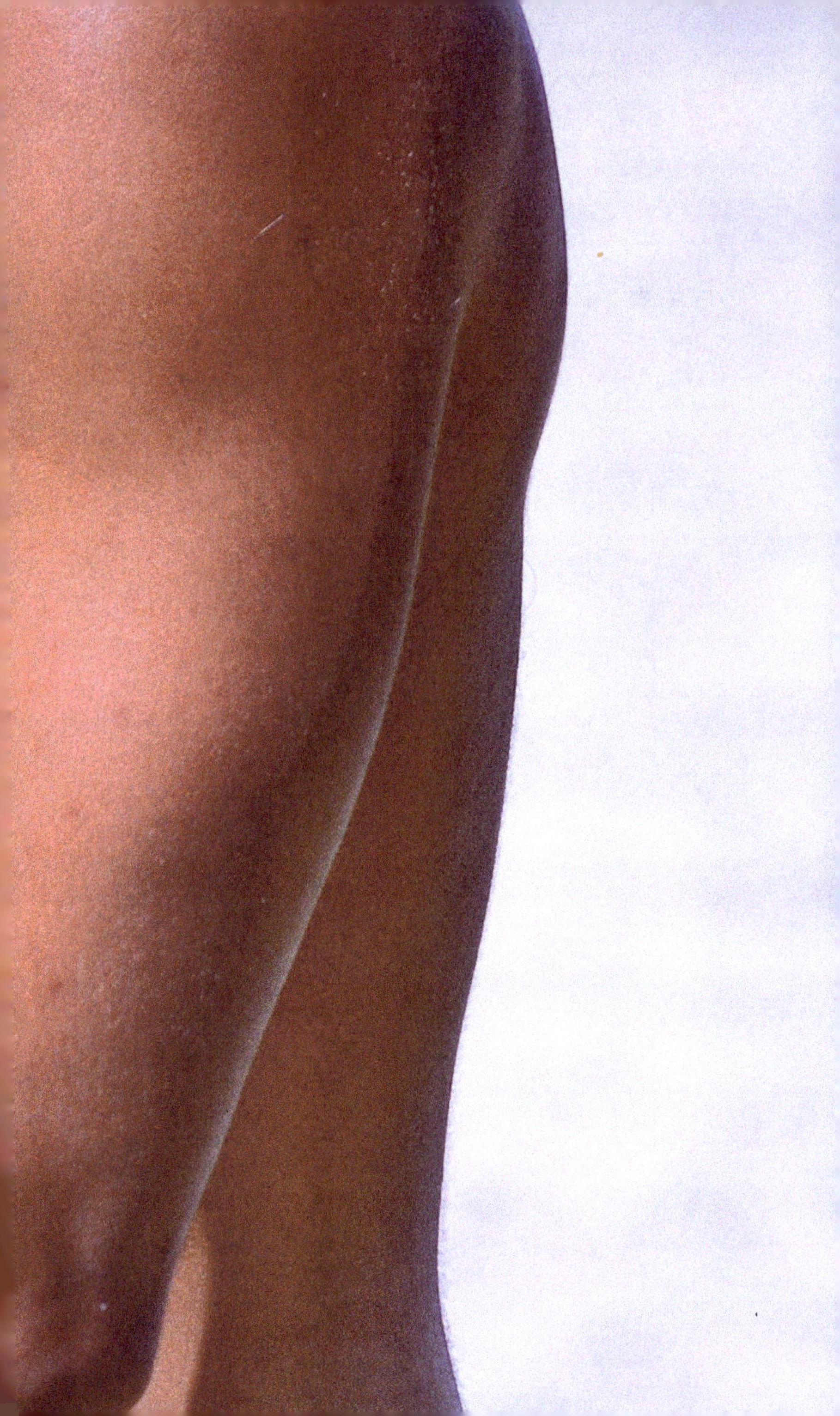

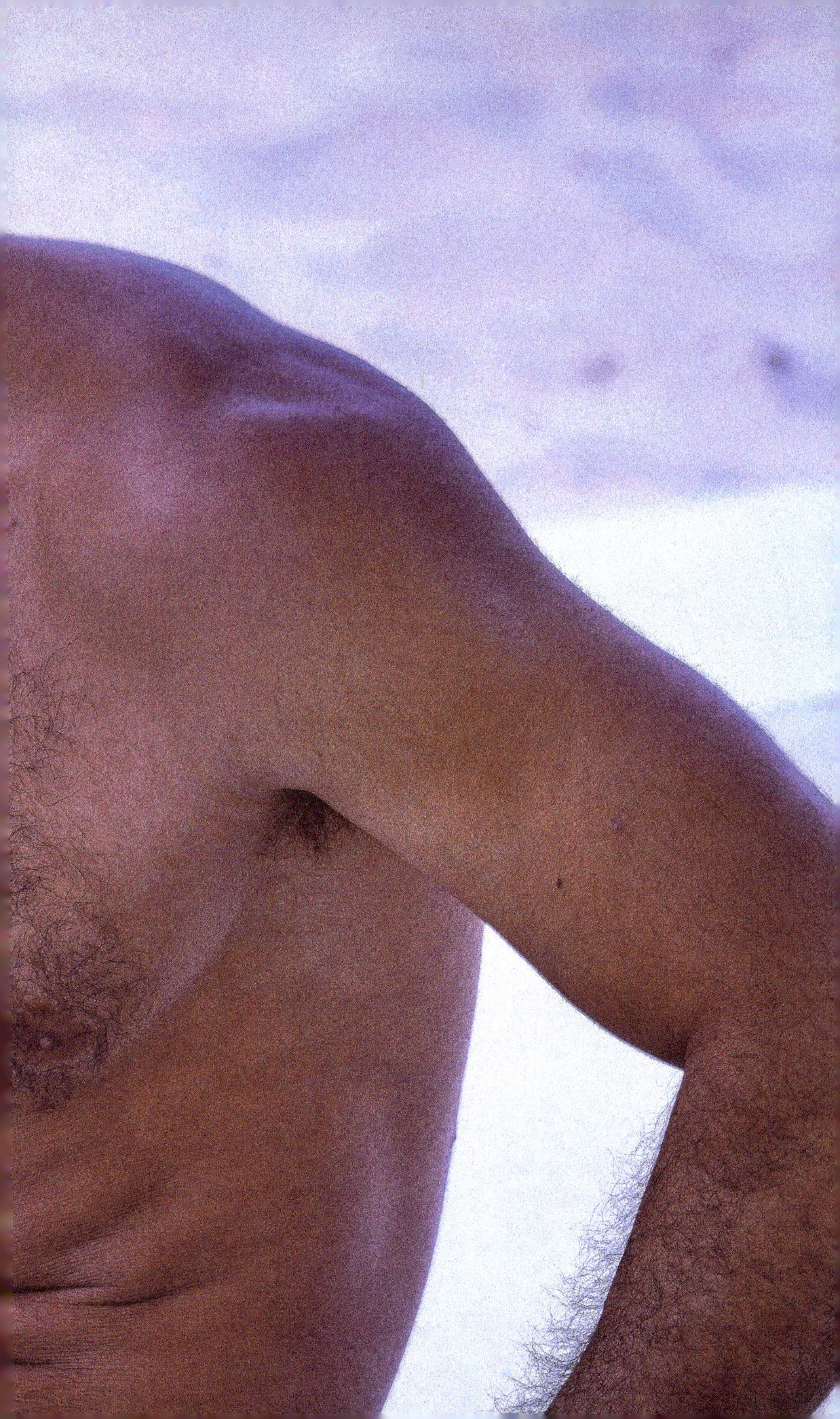

116

16
15

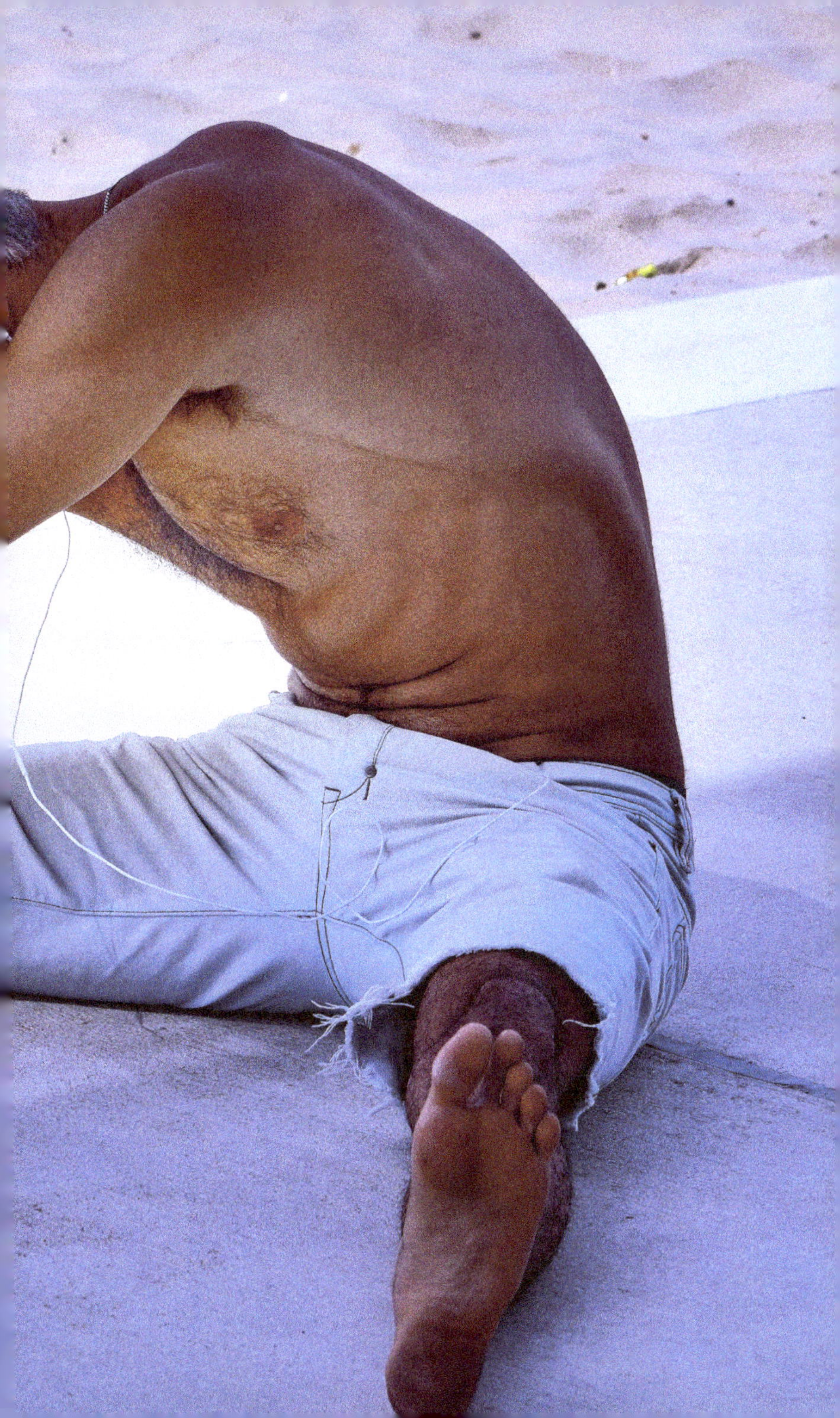

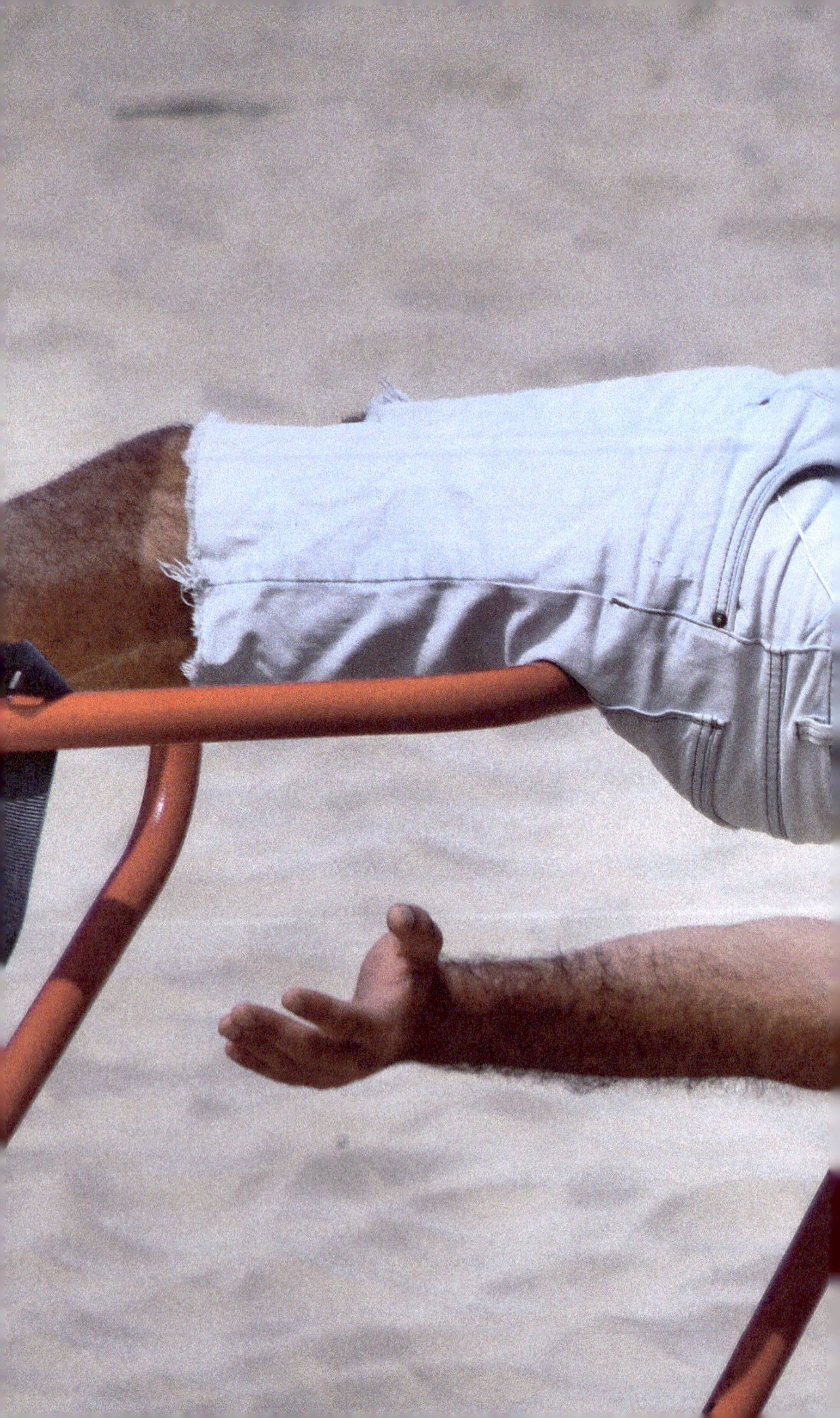

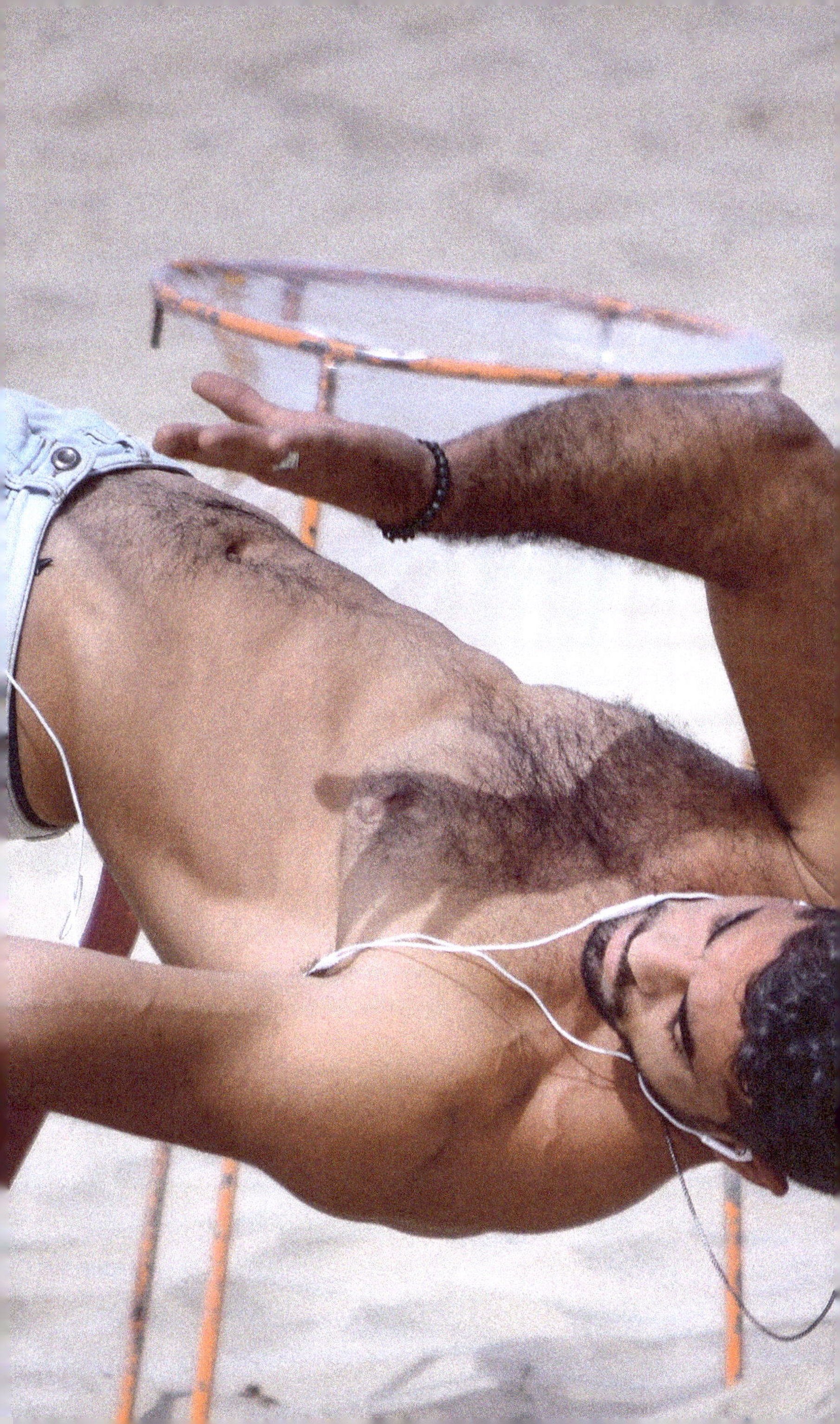

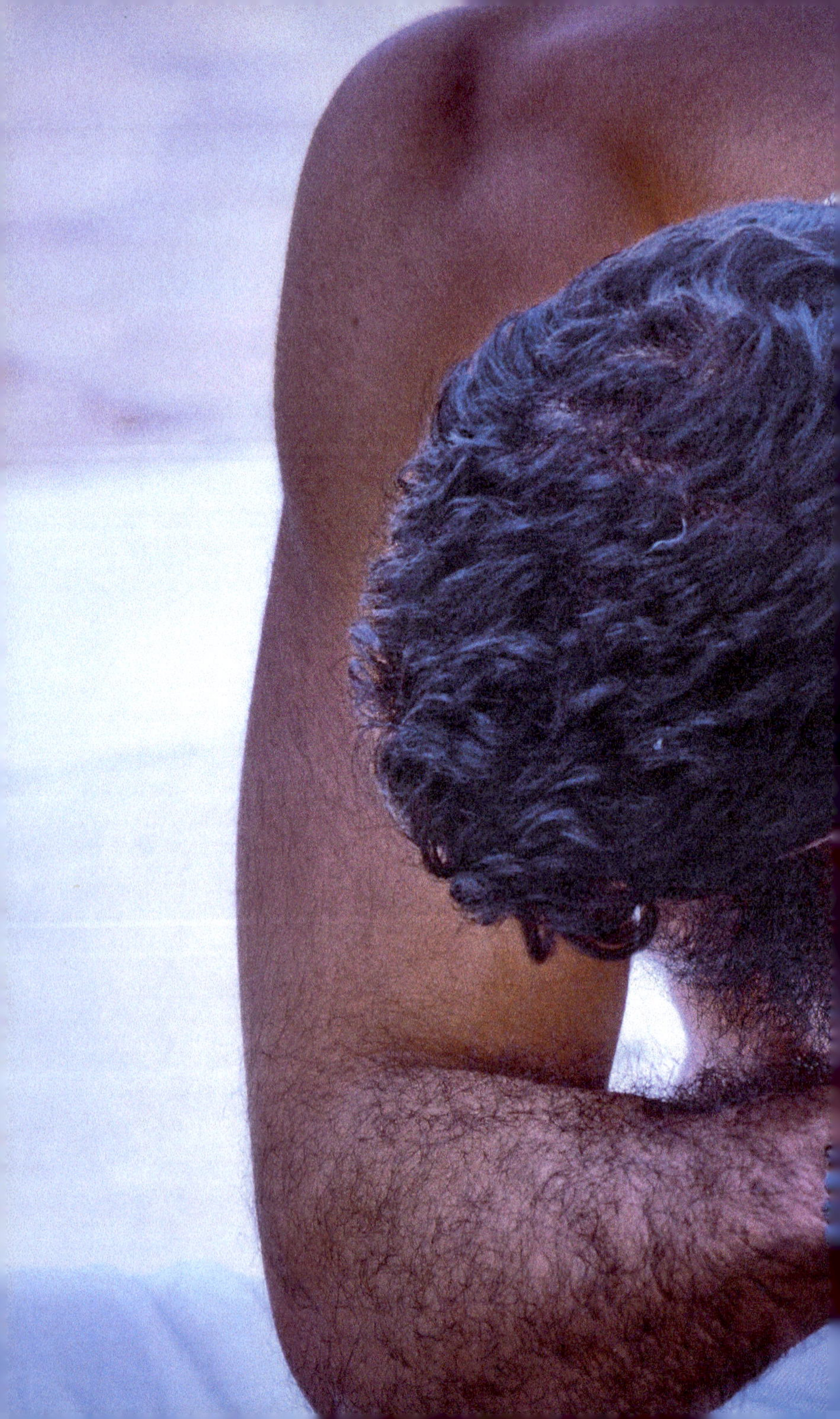

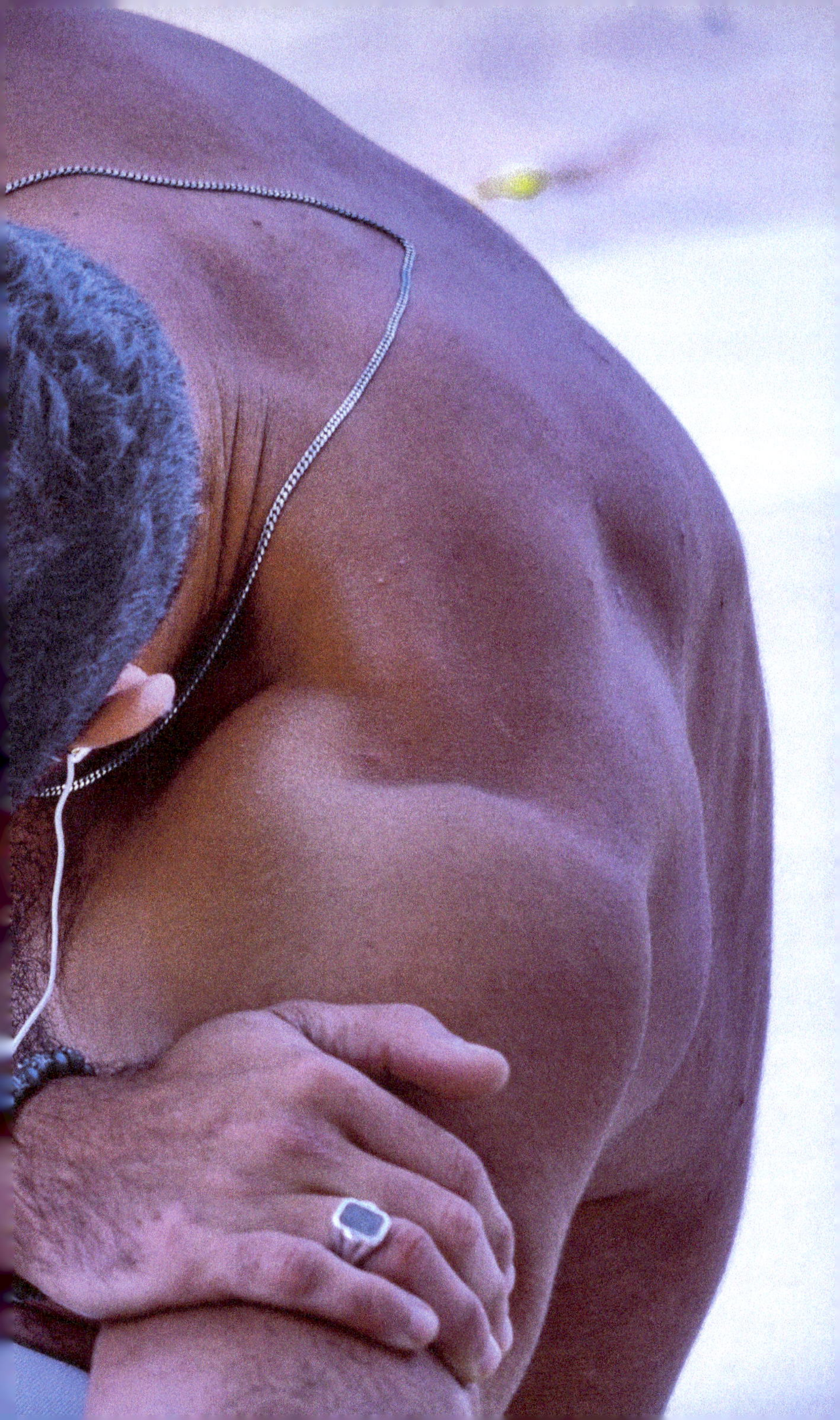

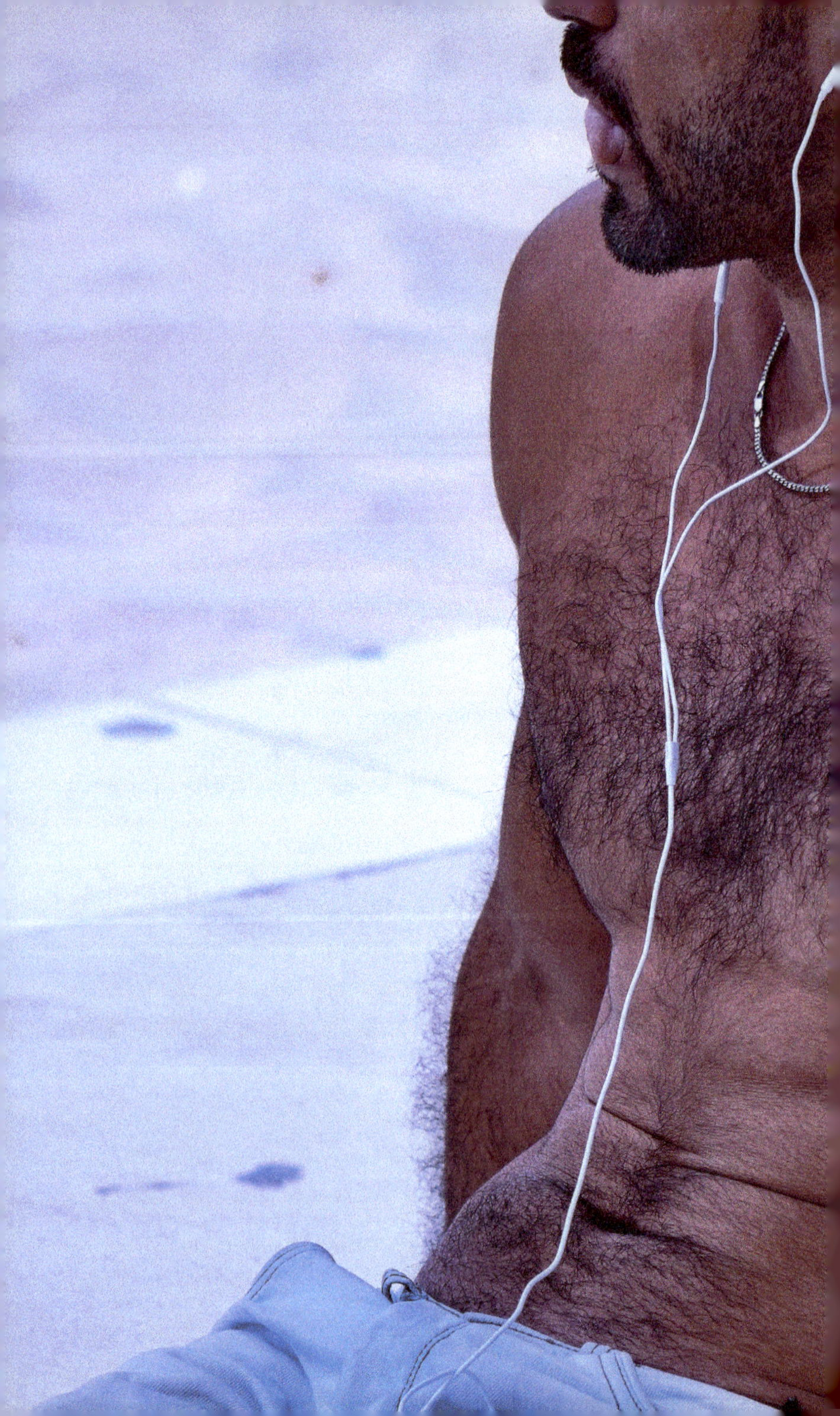

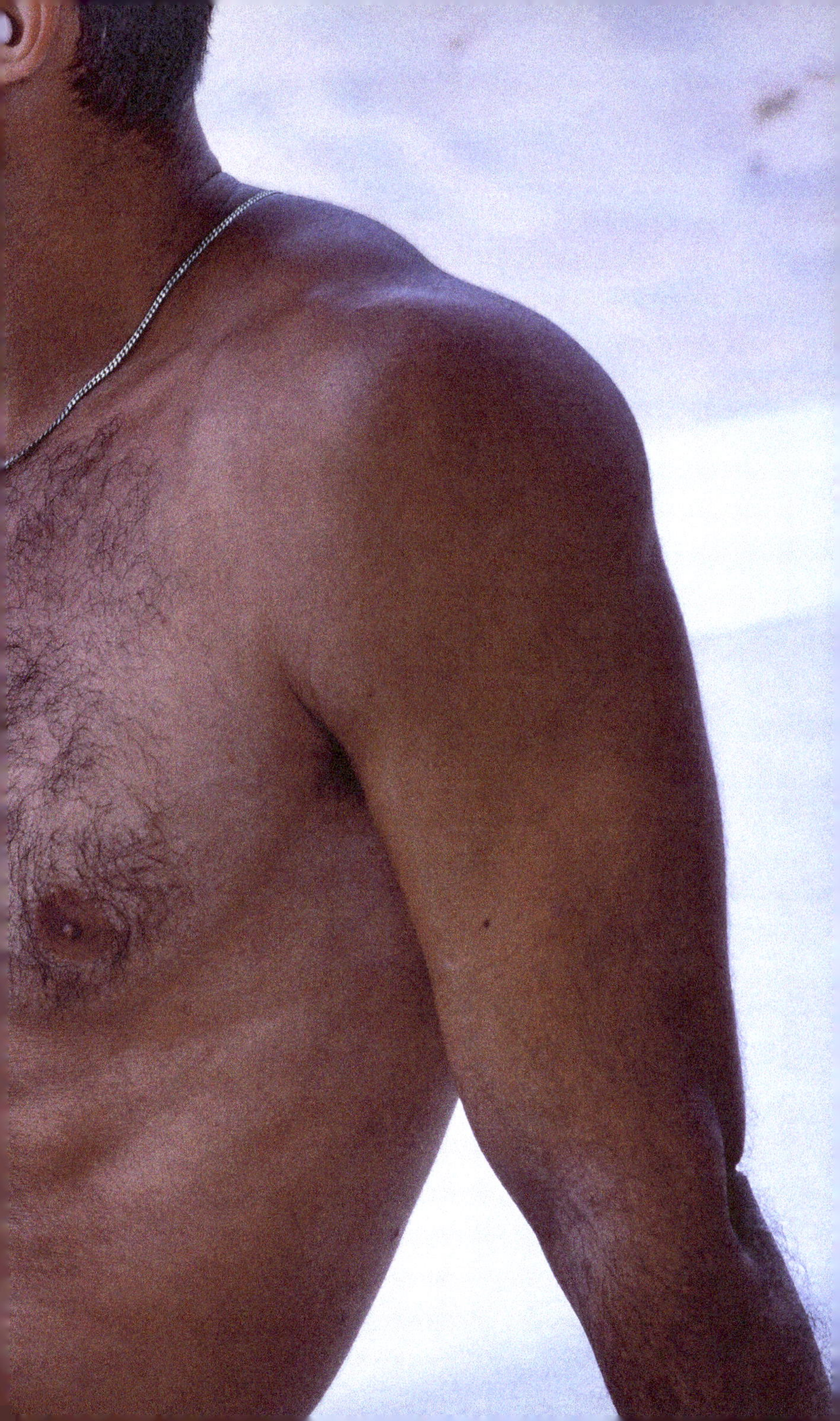

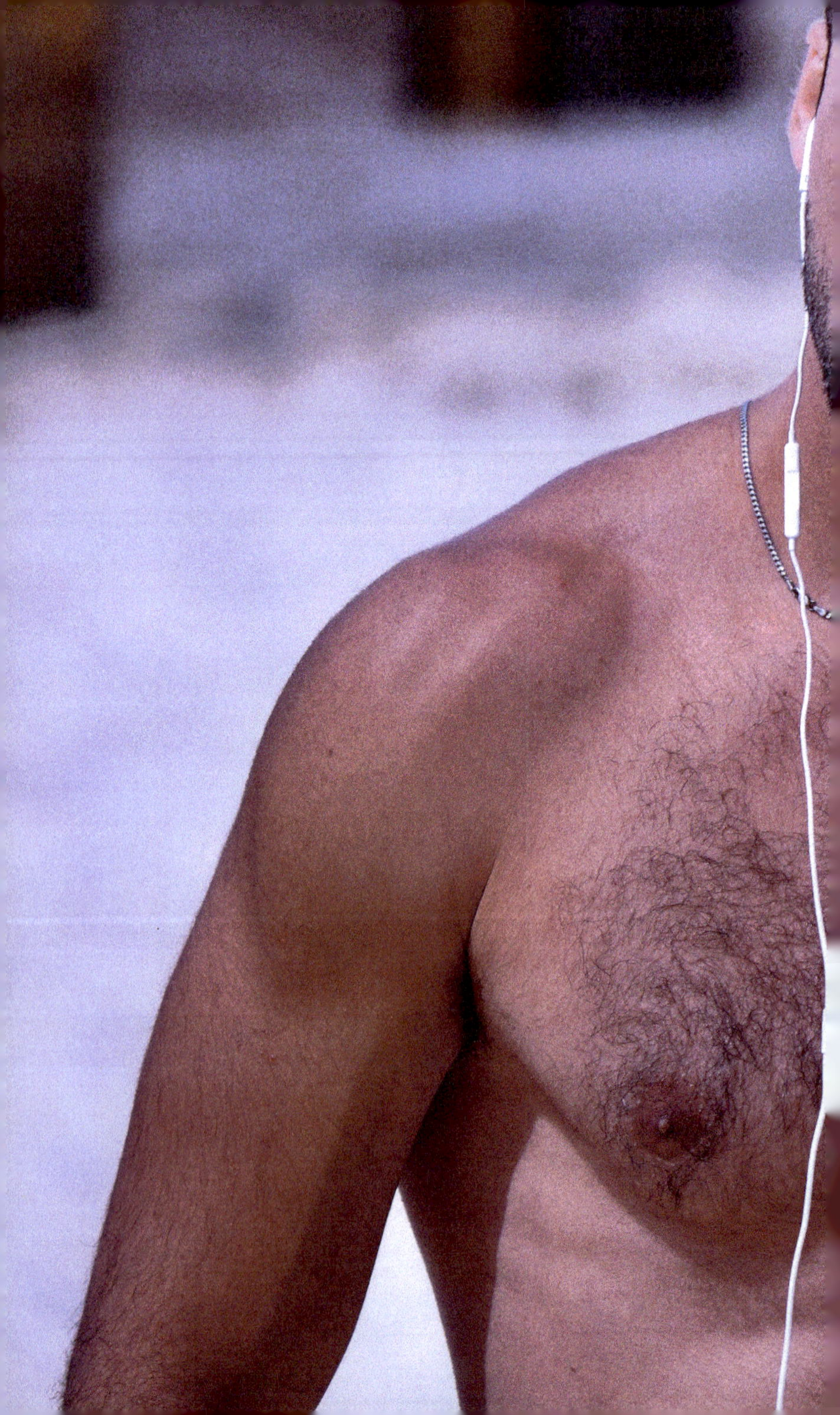

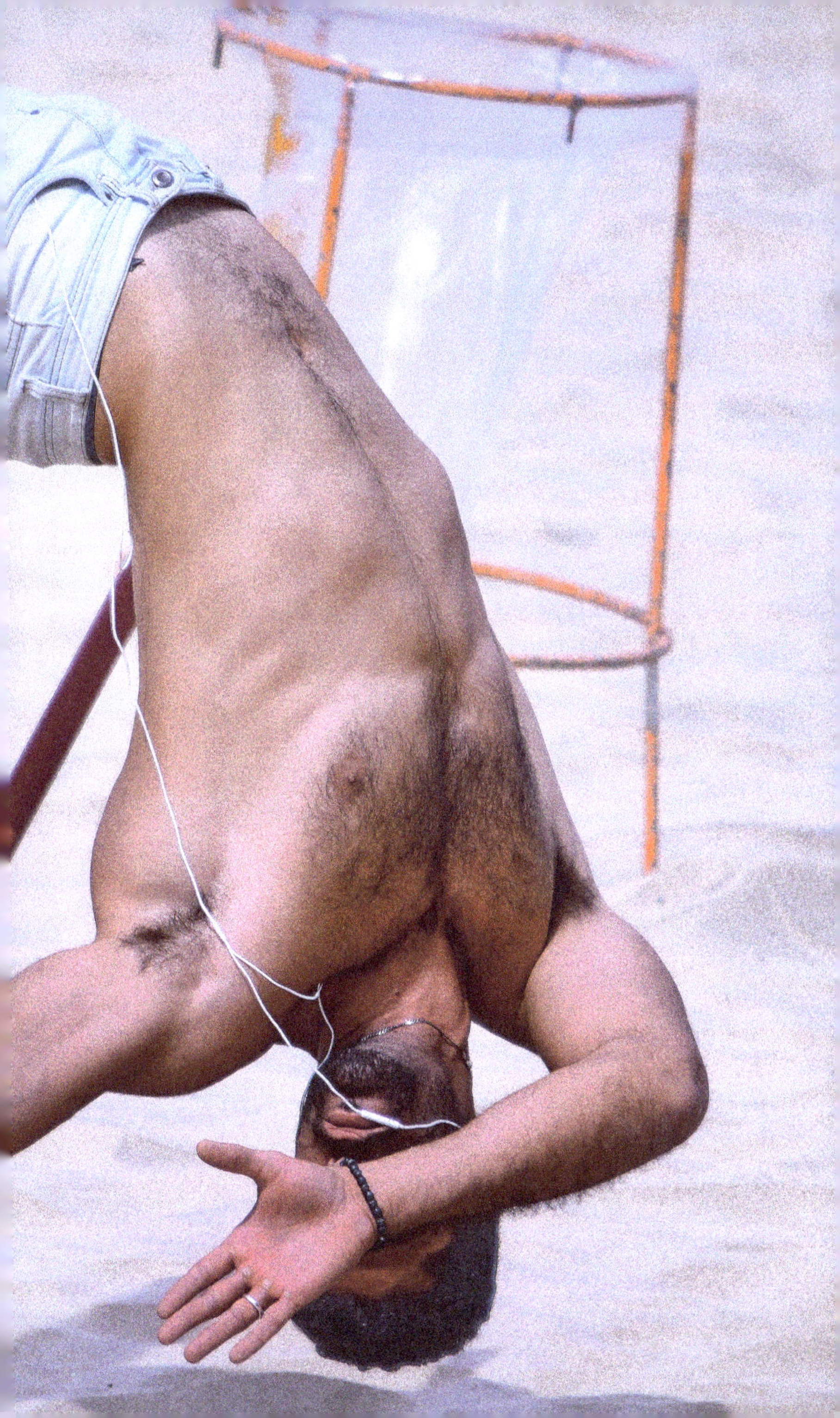

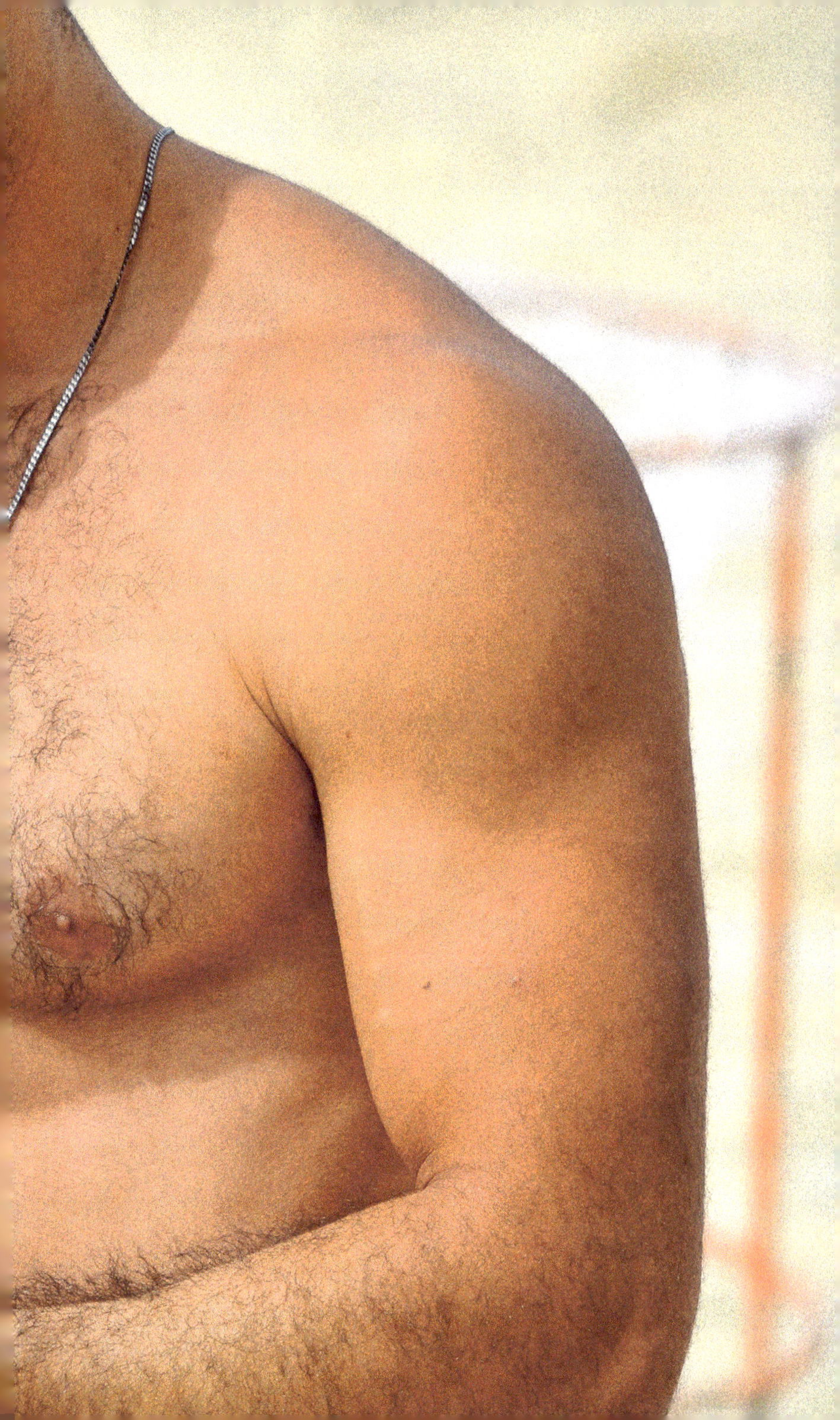

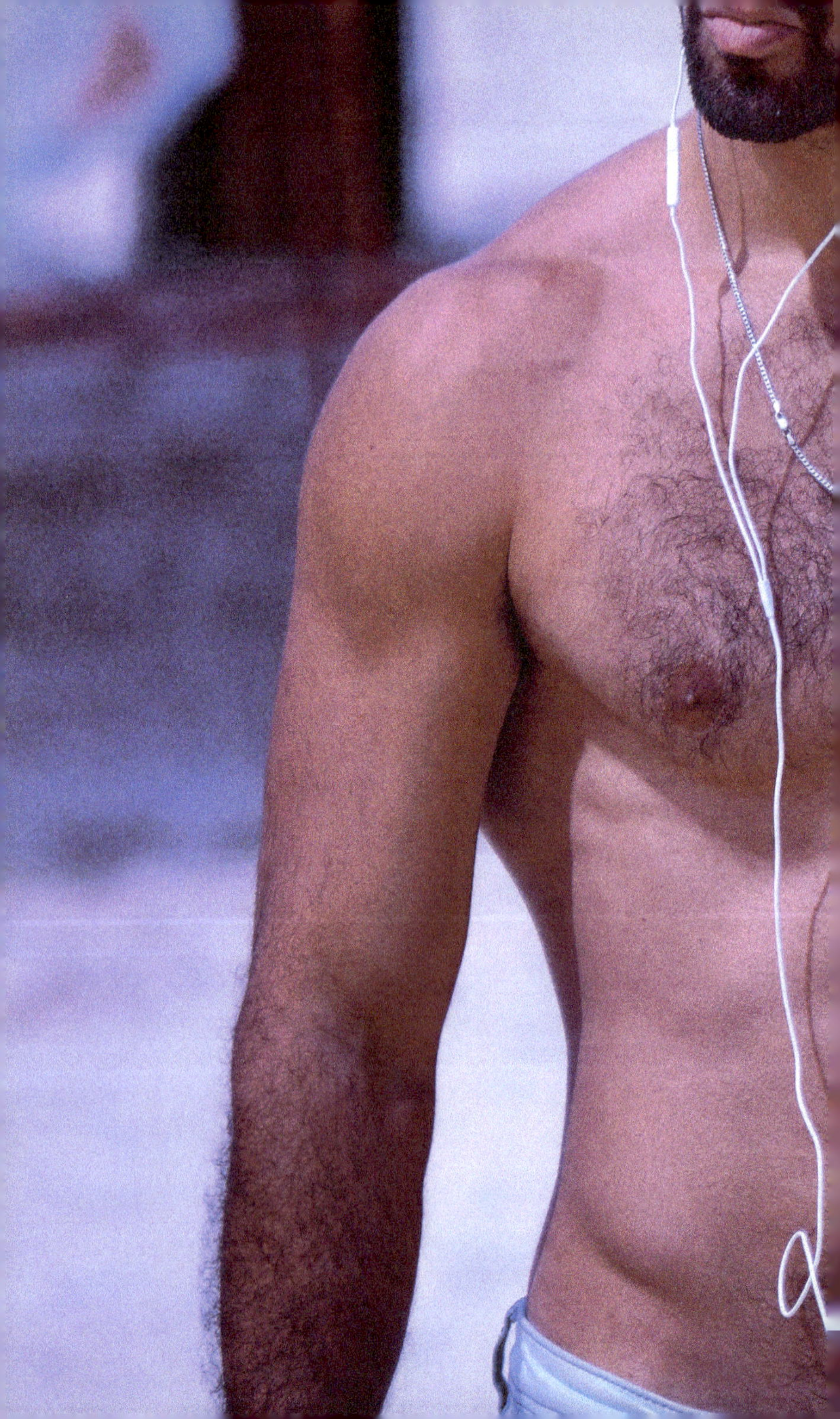

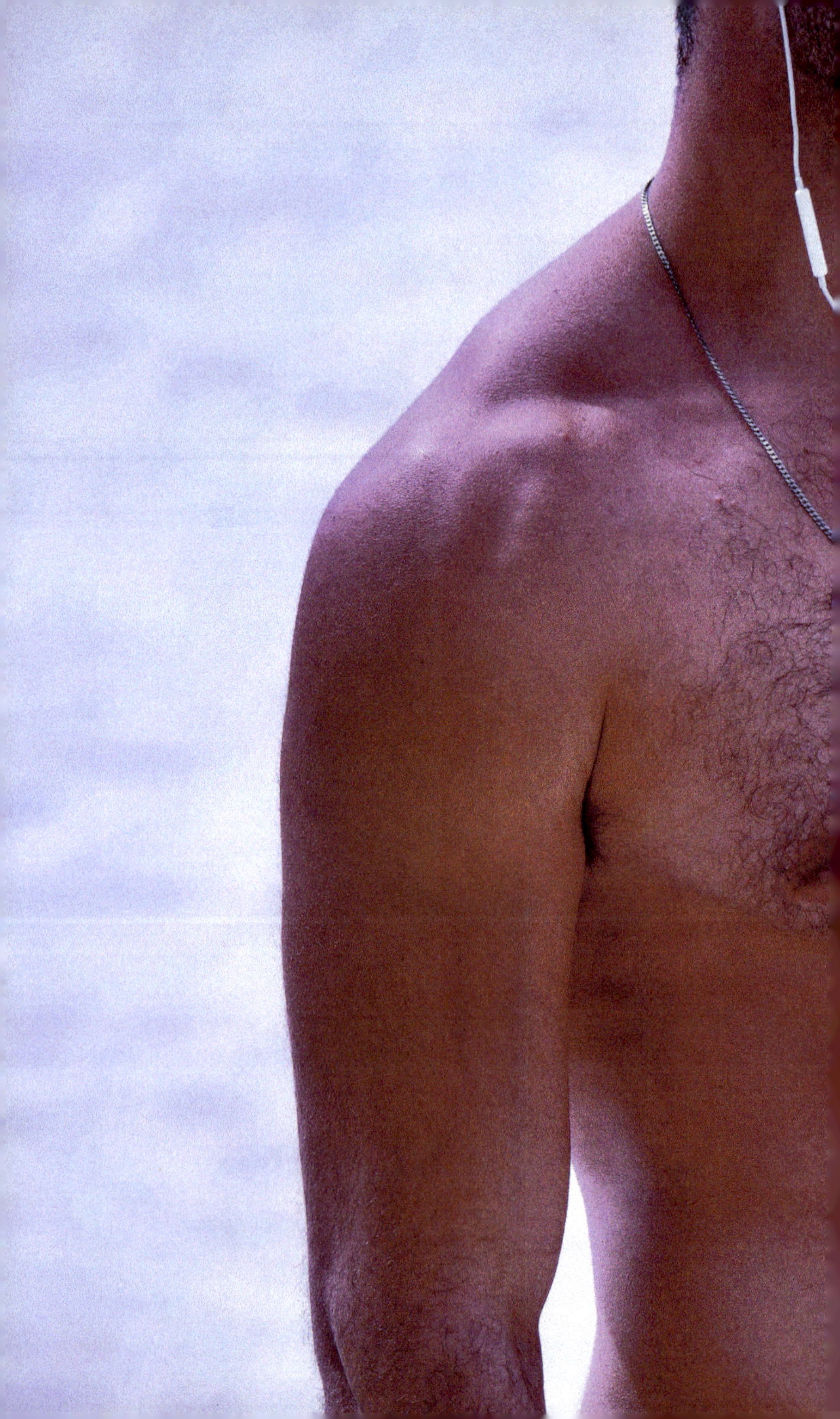

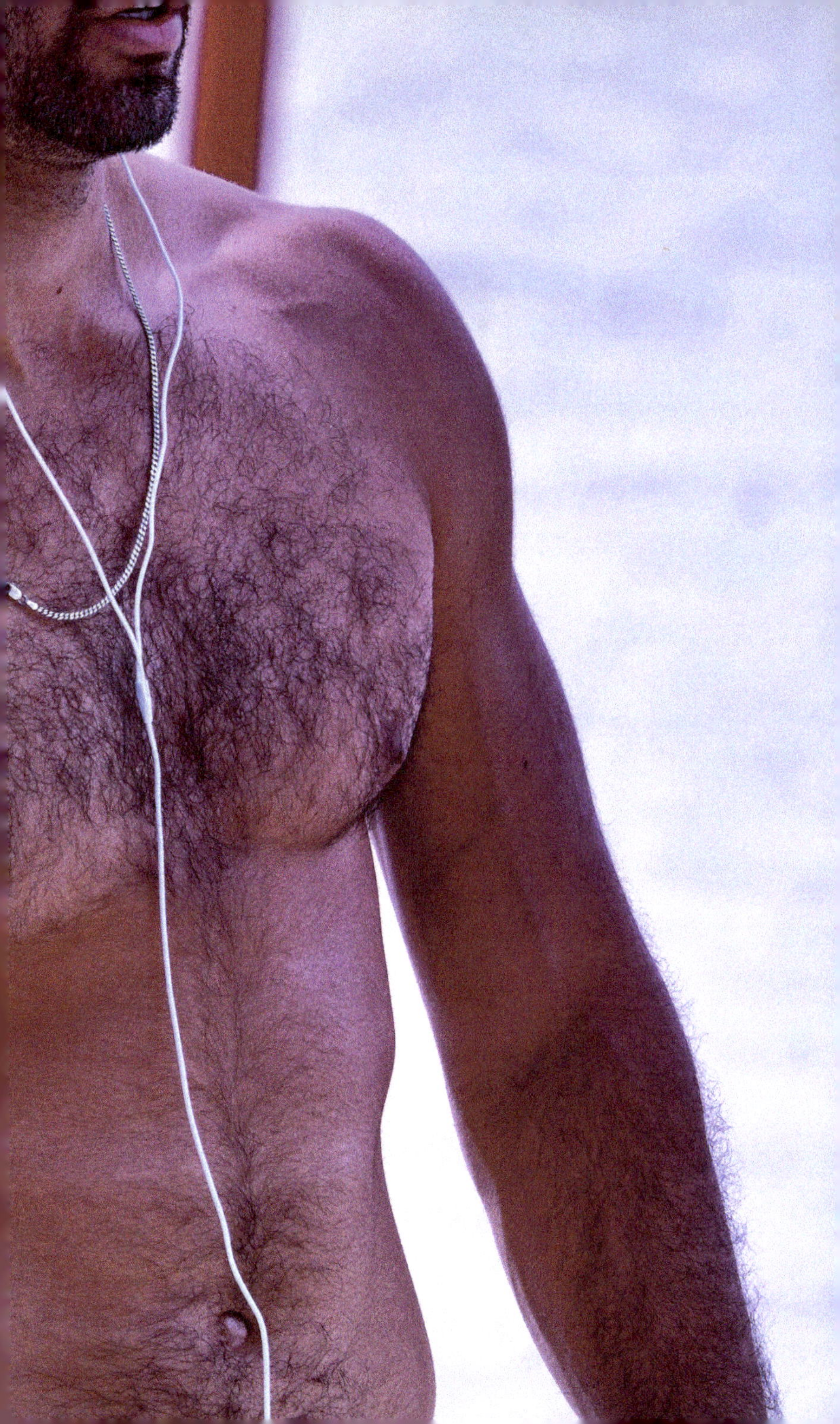

116

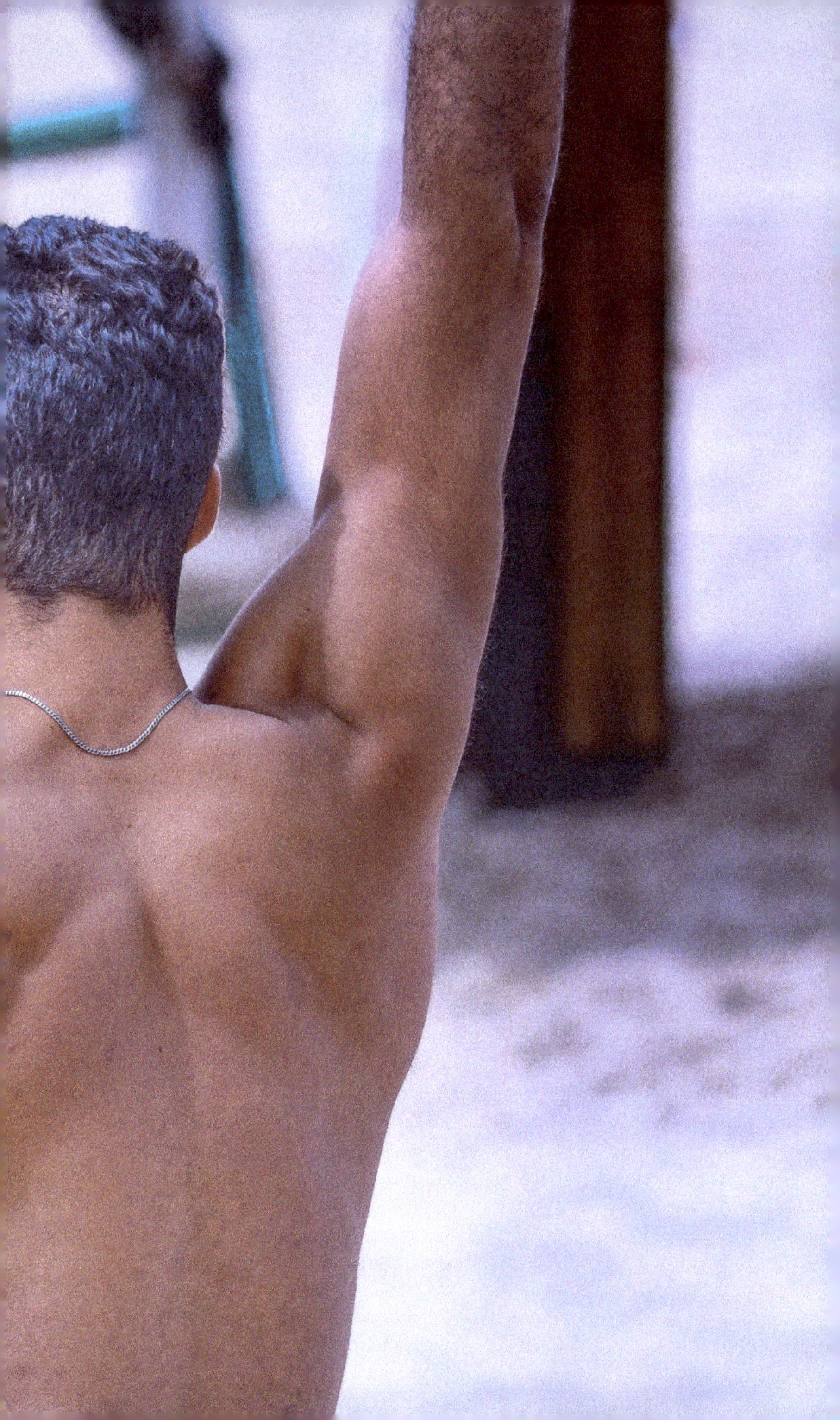

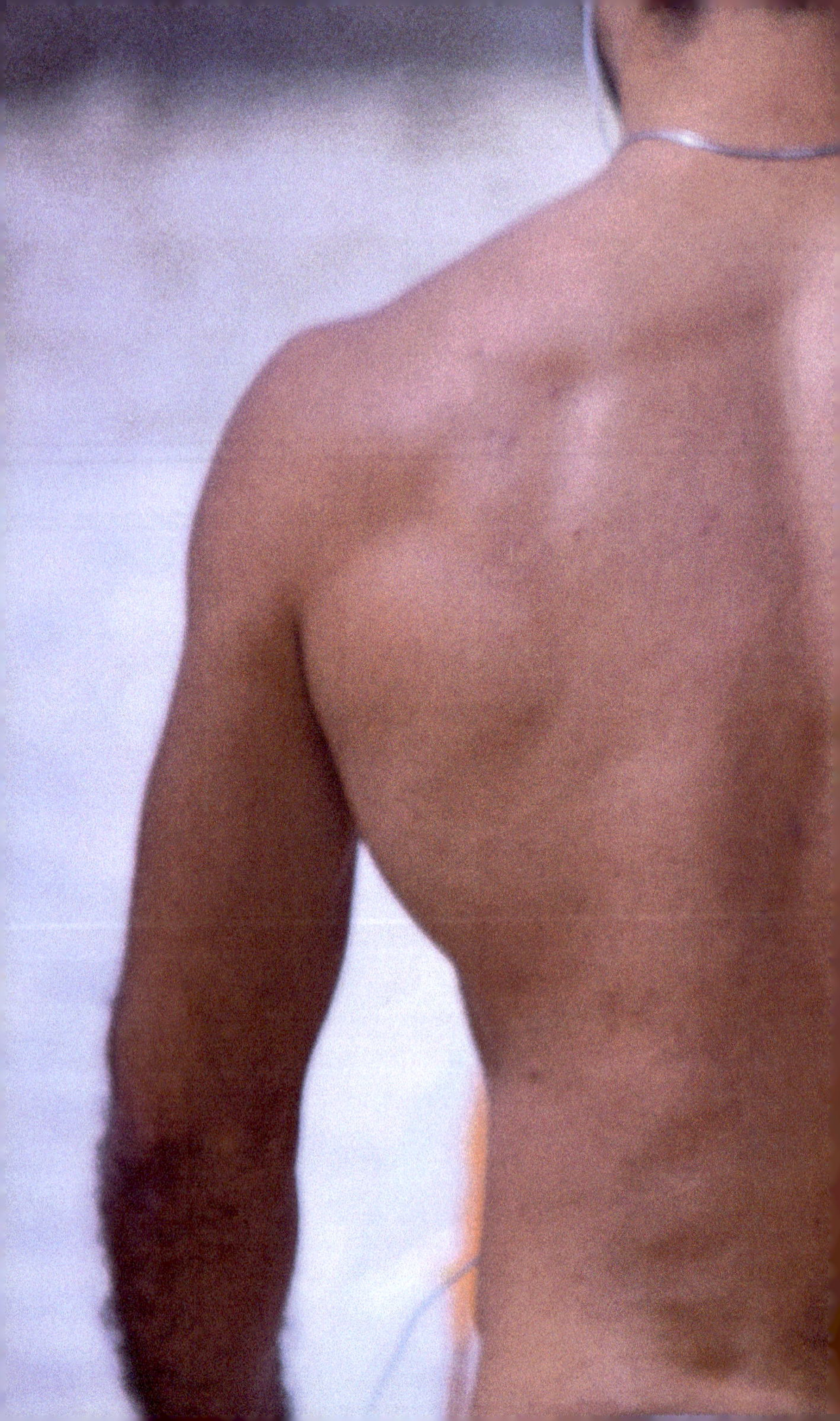

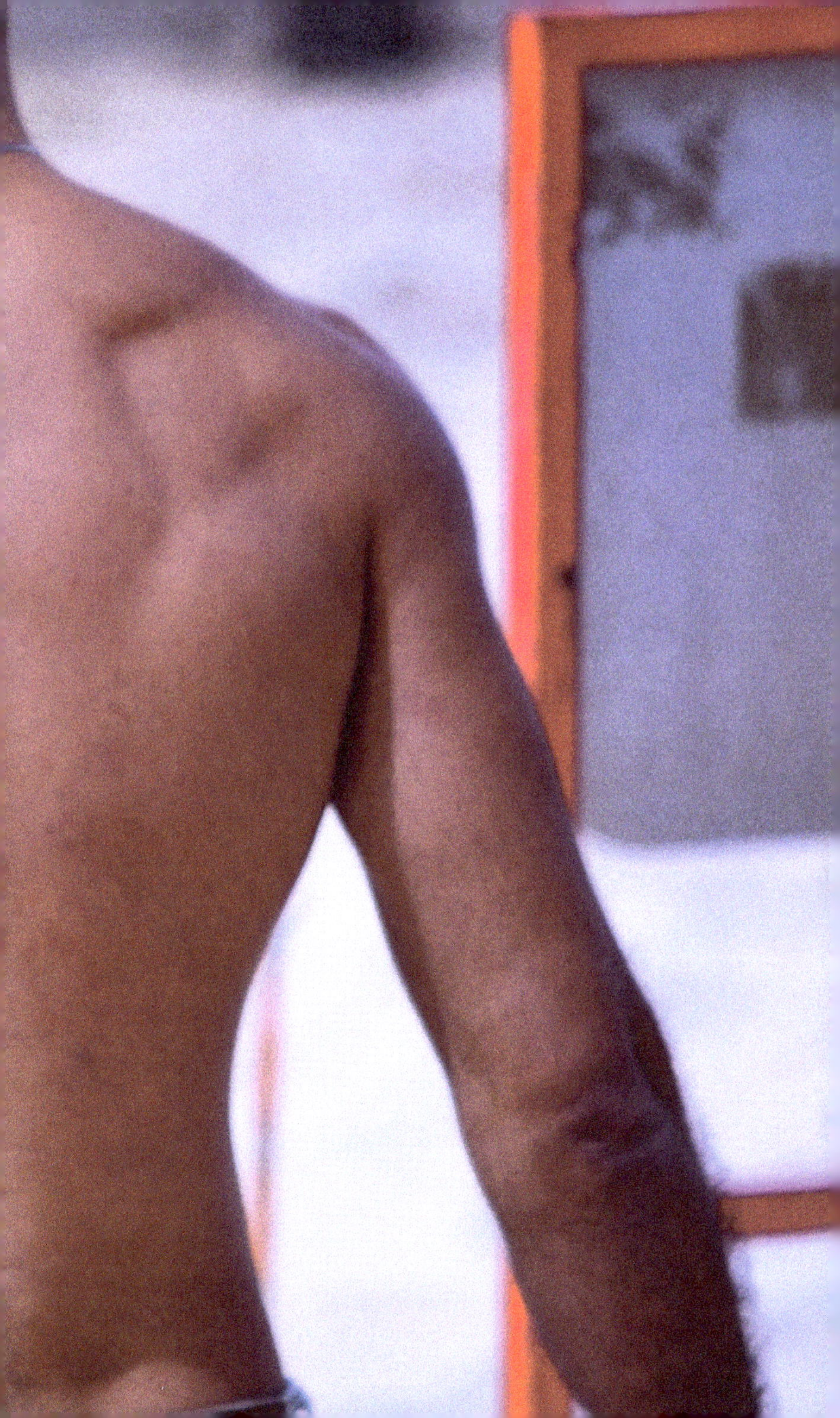

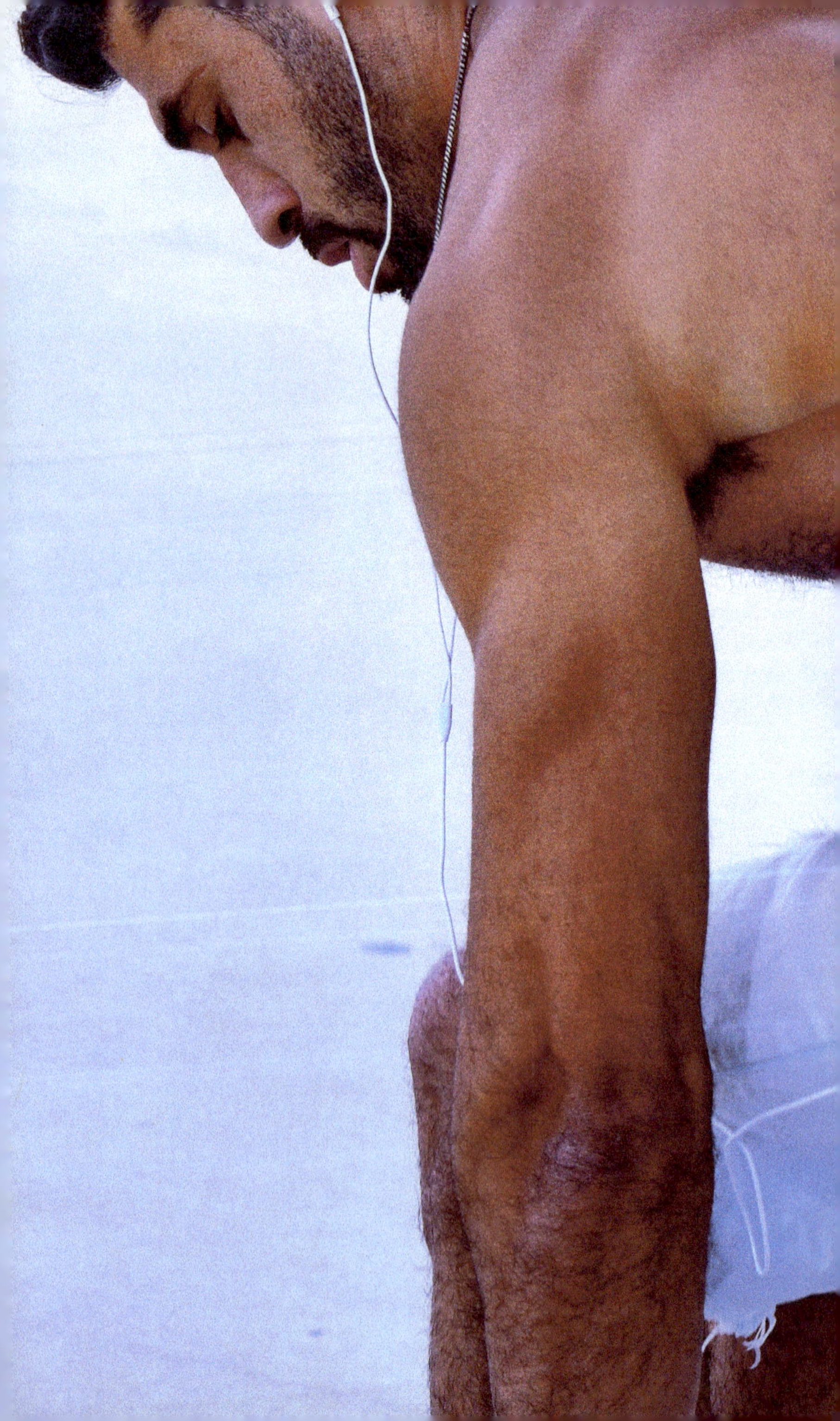

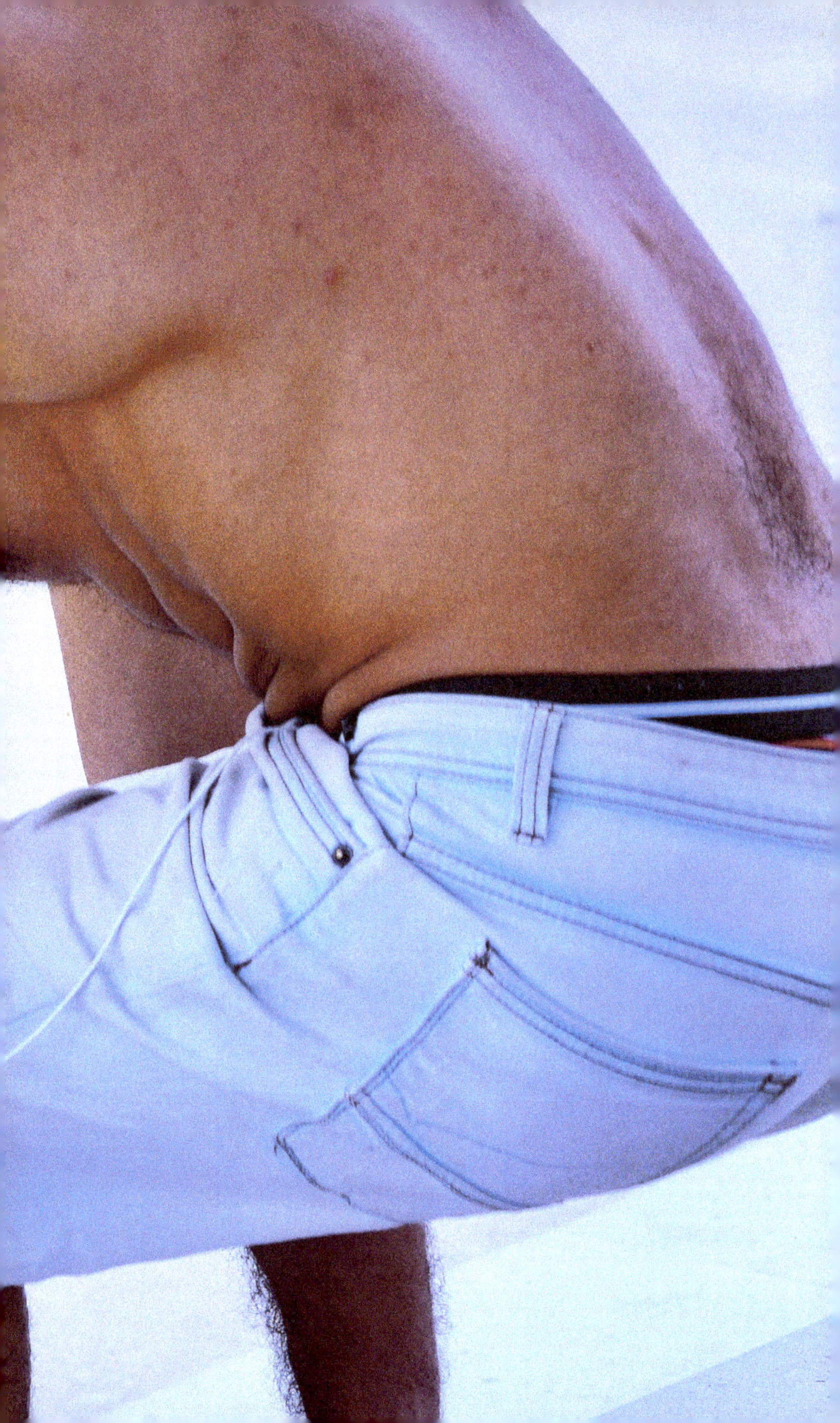

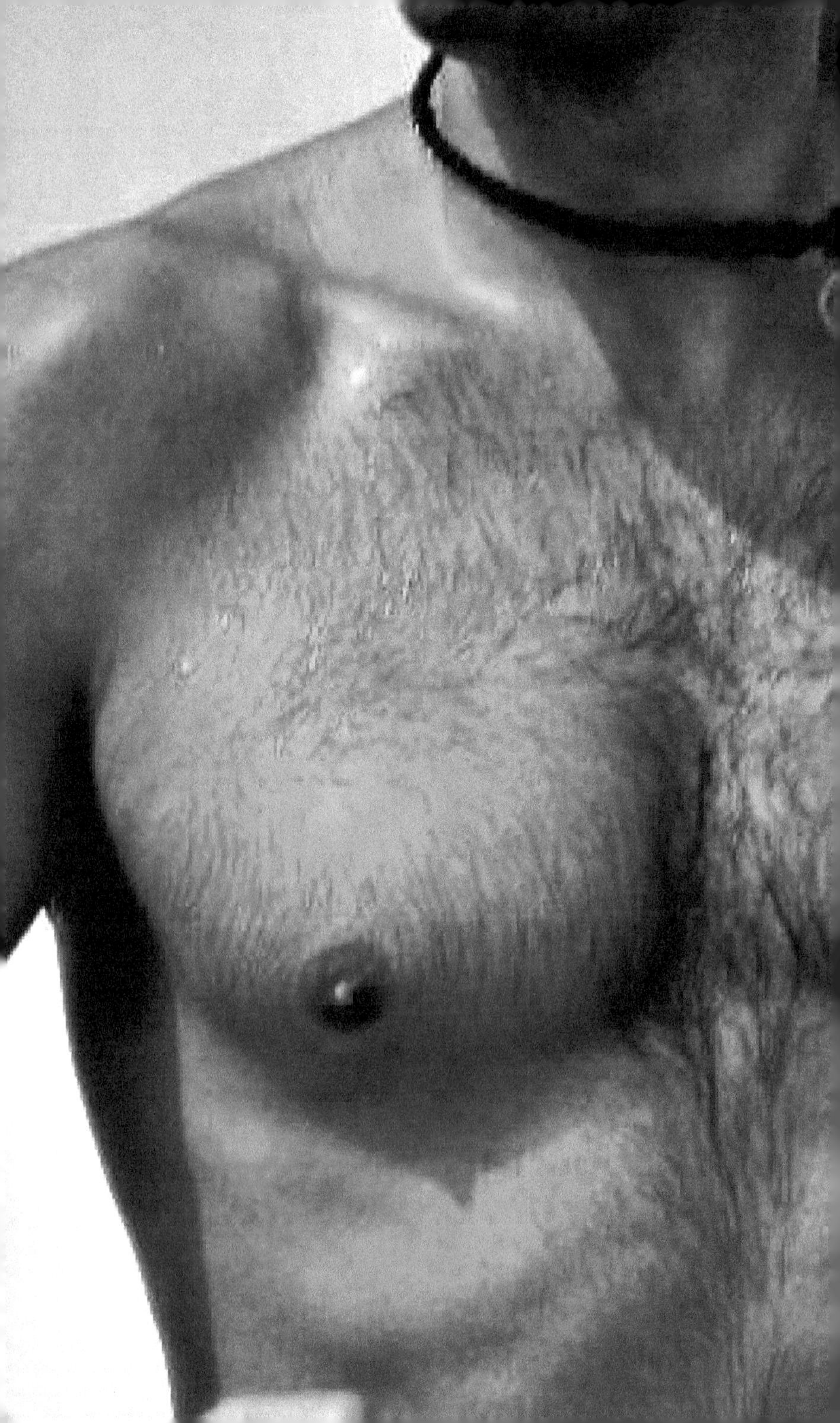

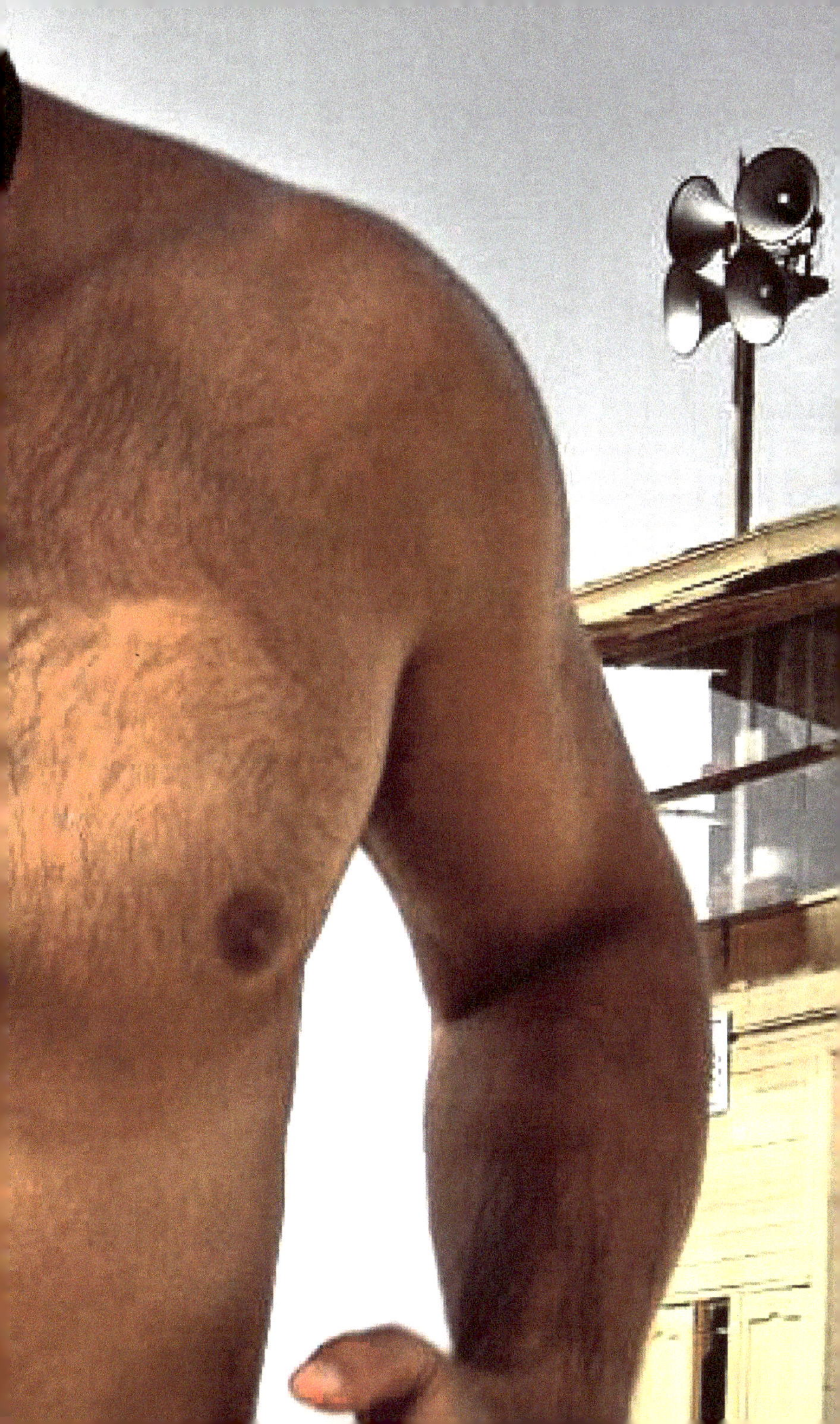

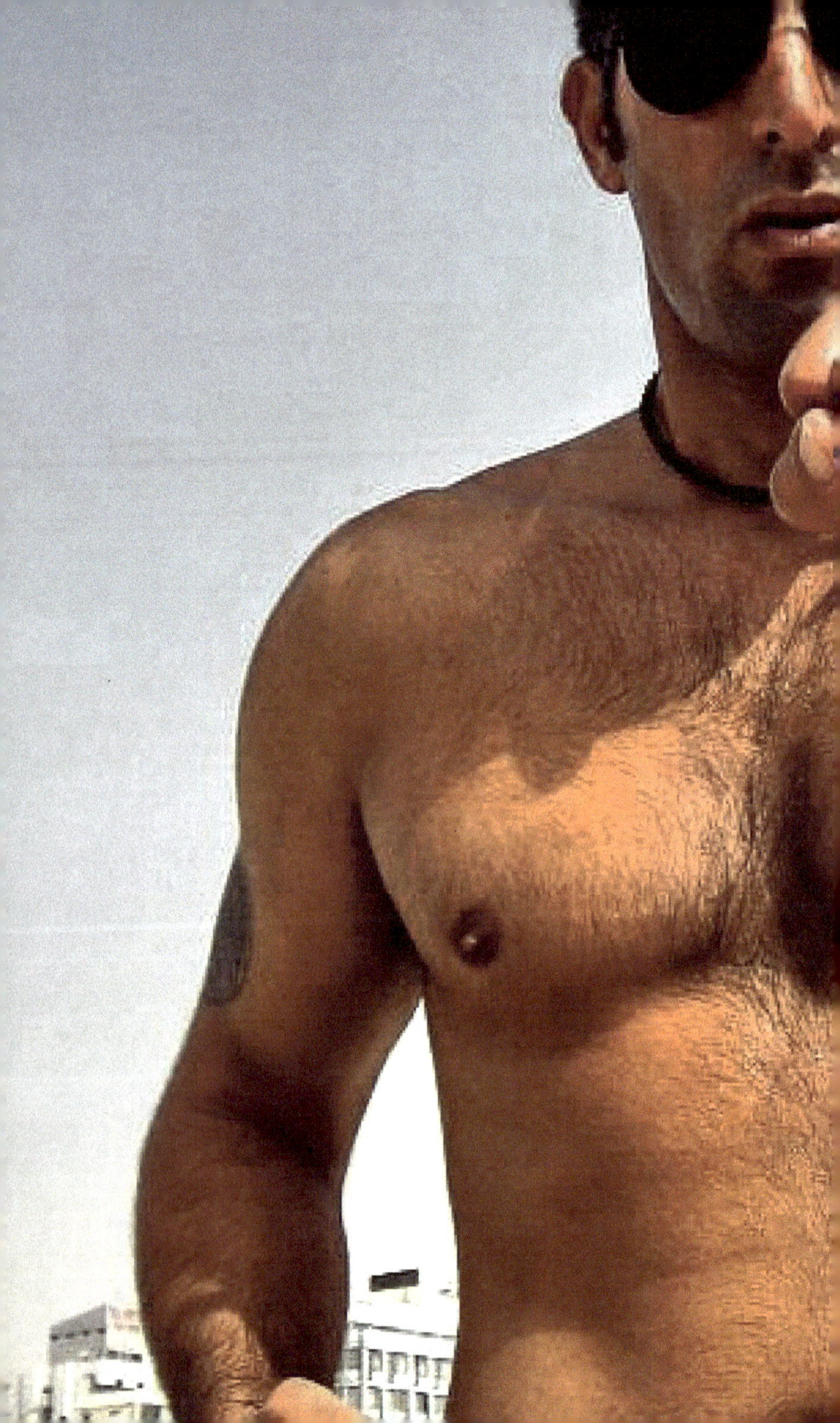

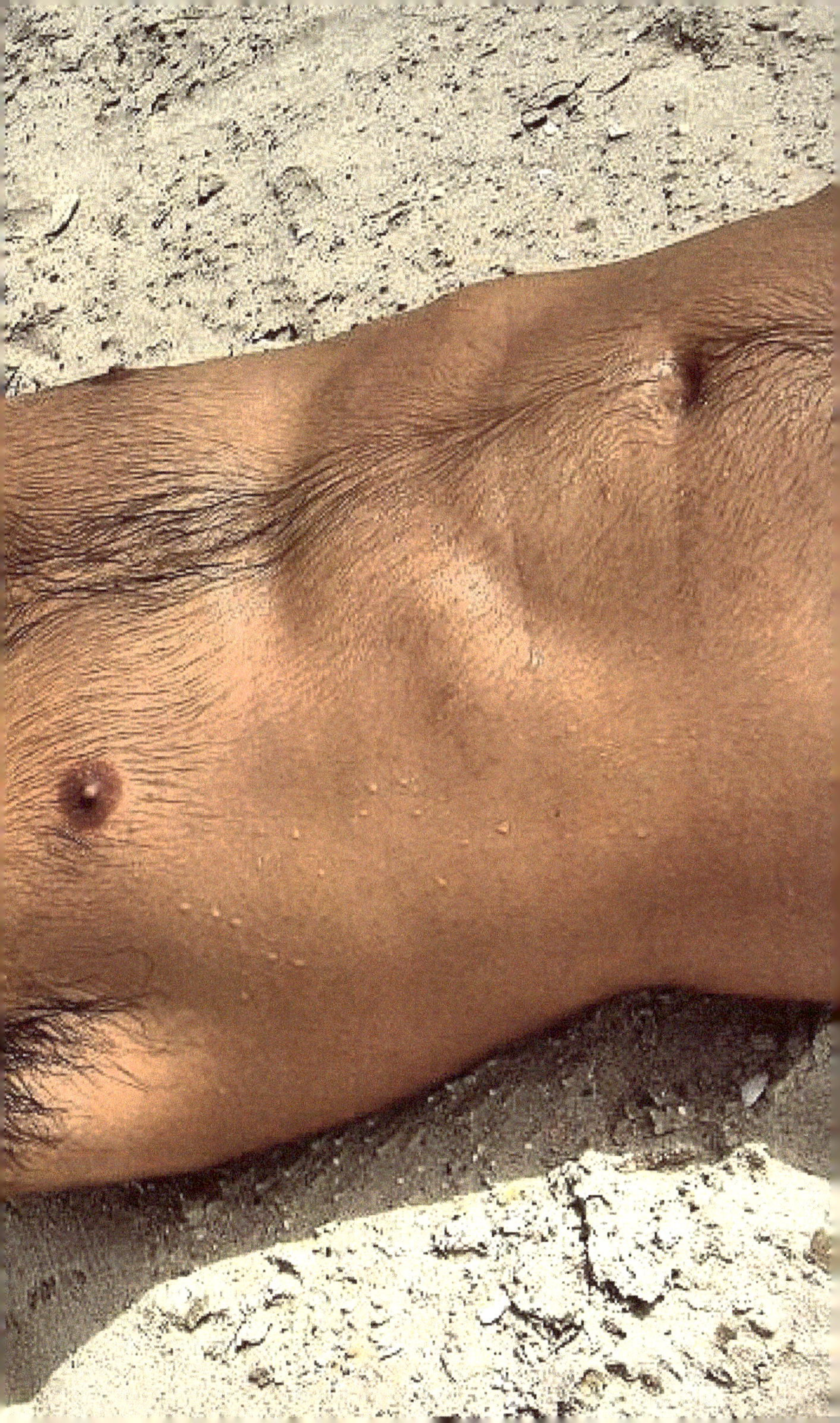

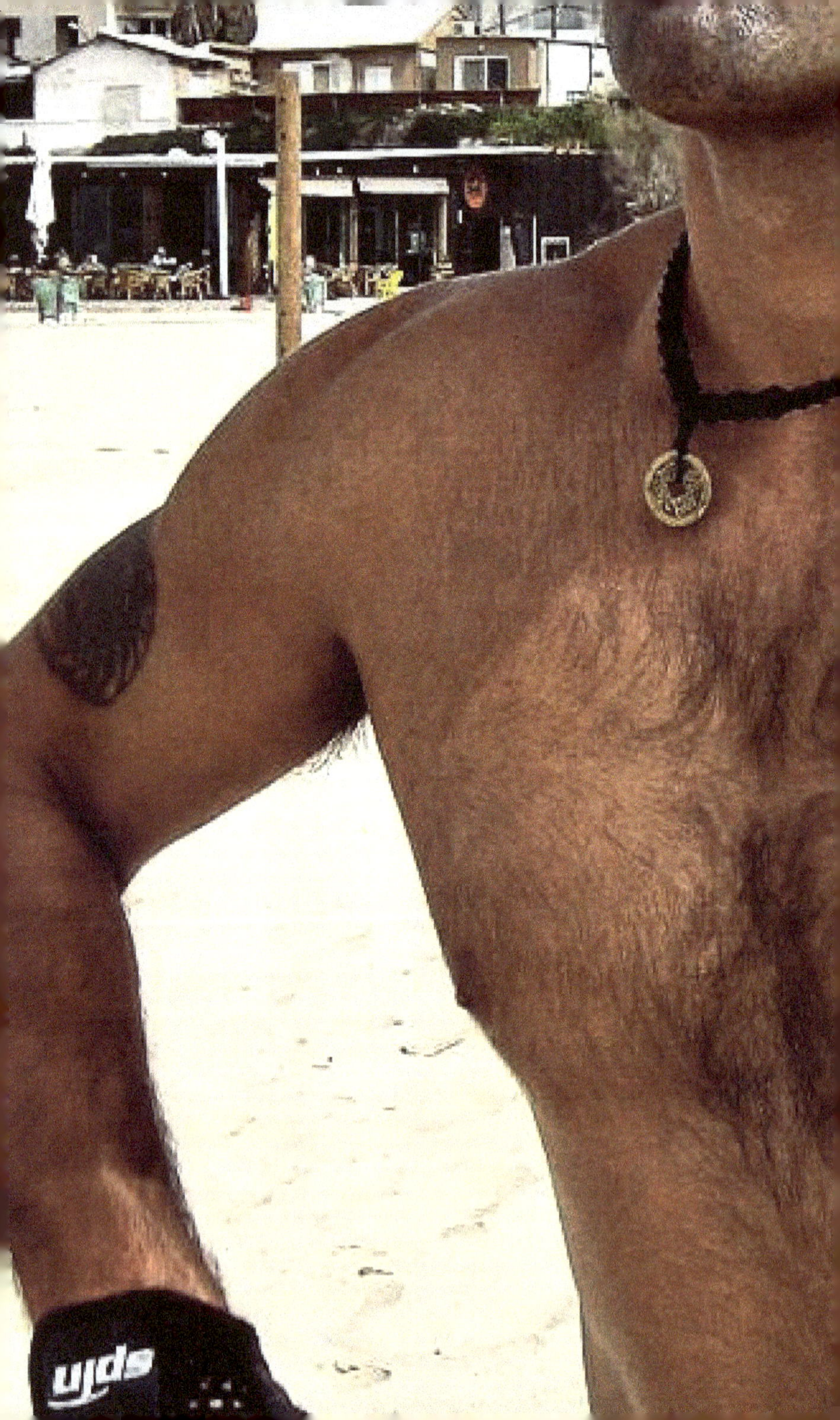

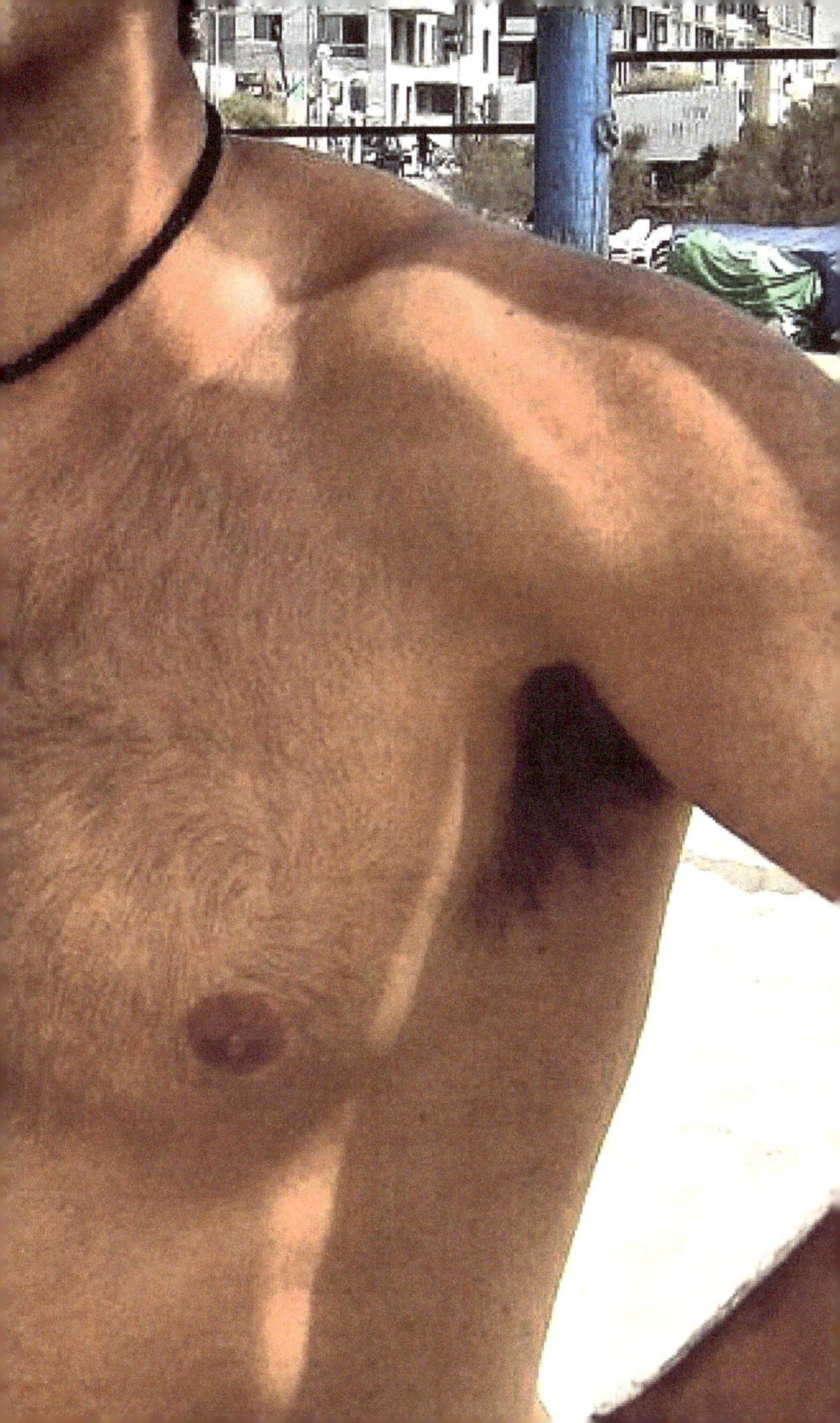

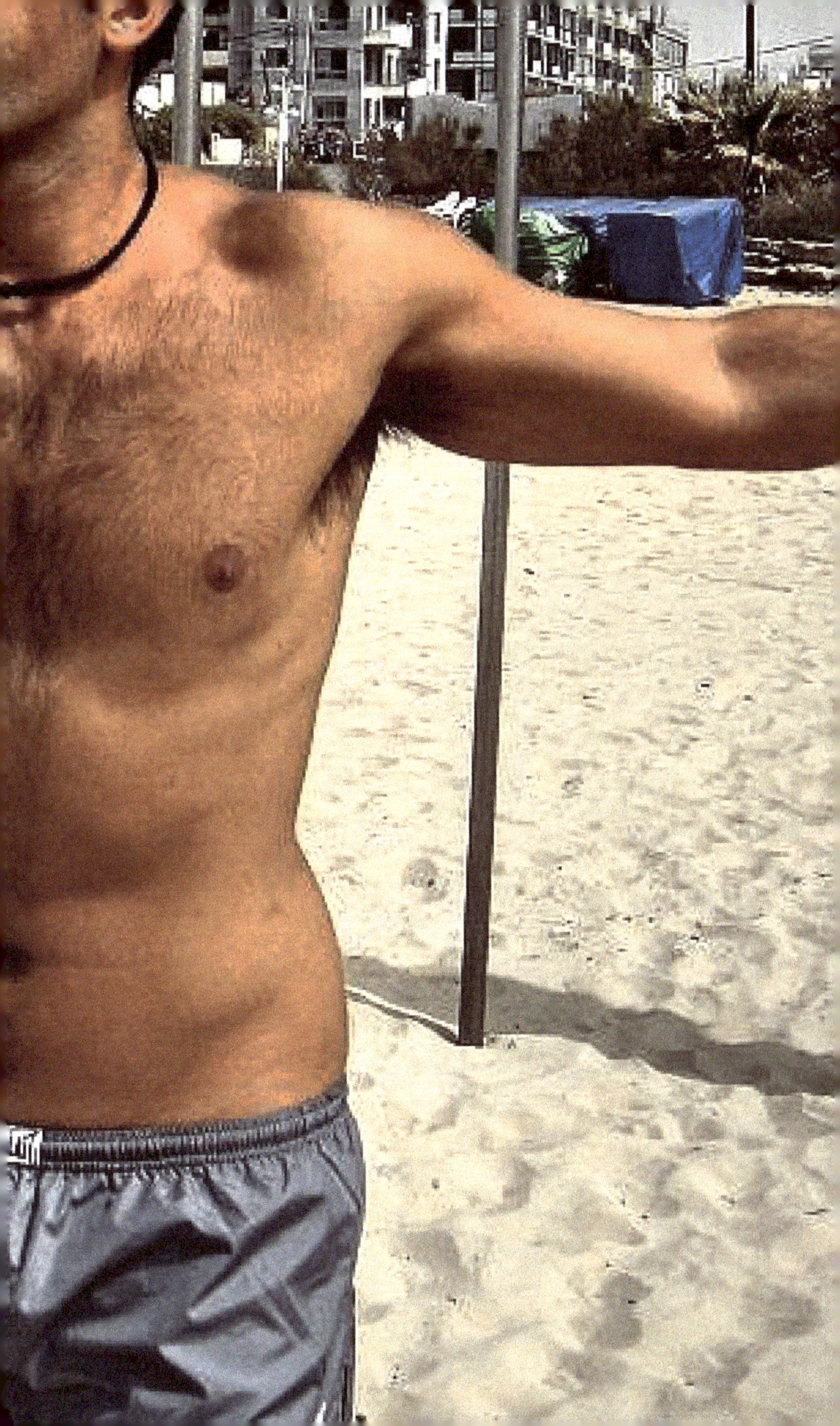

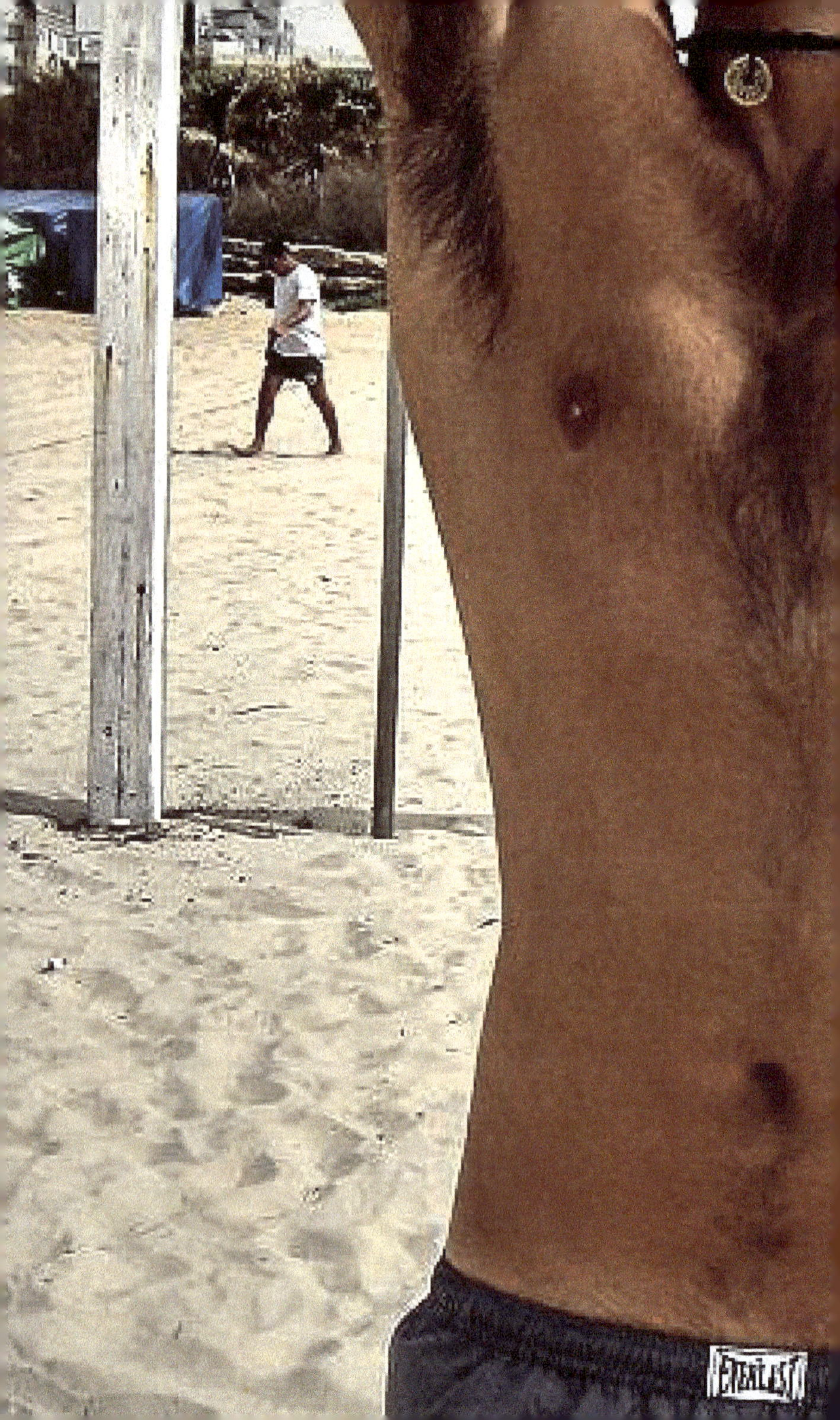

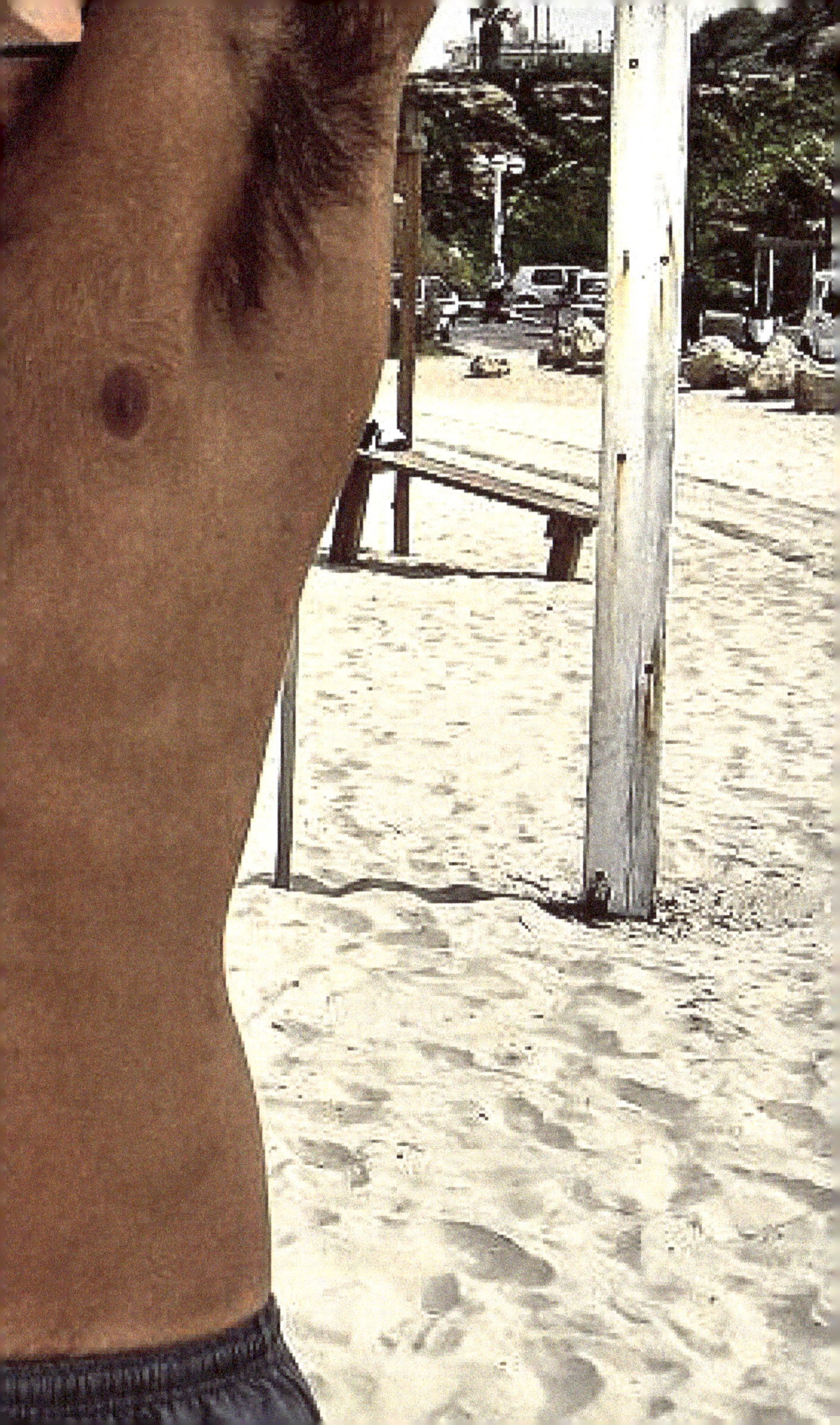

EVERLA

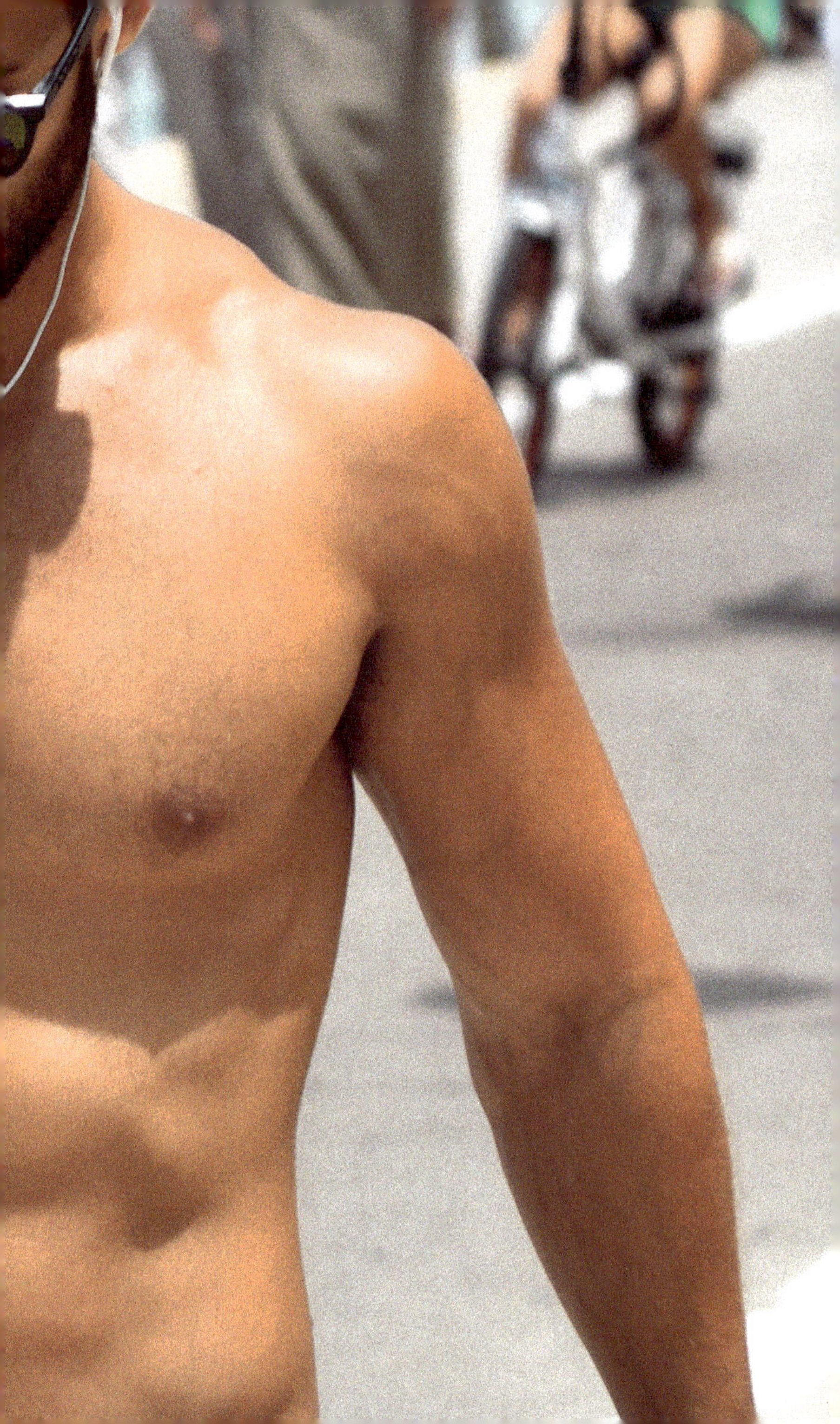

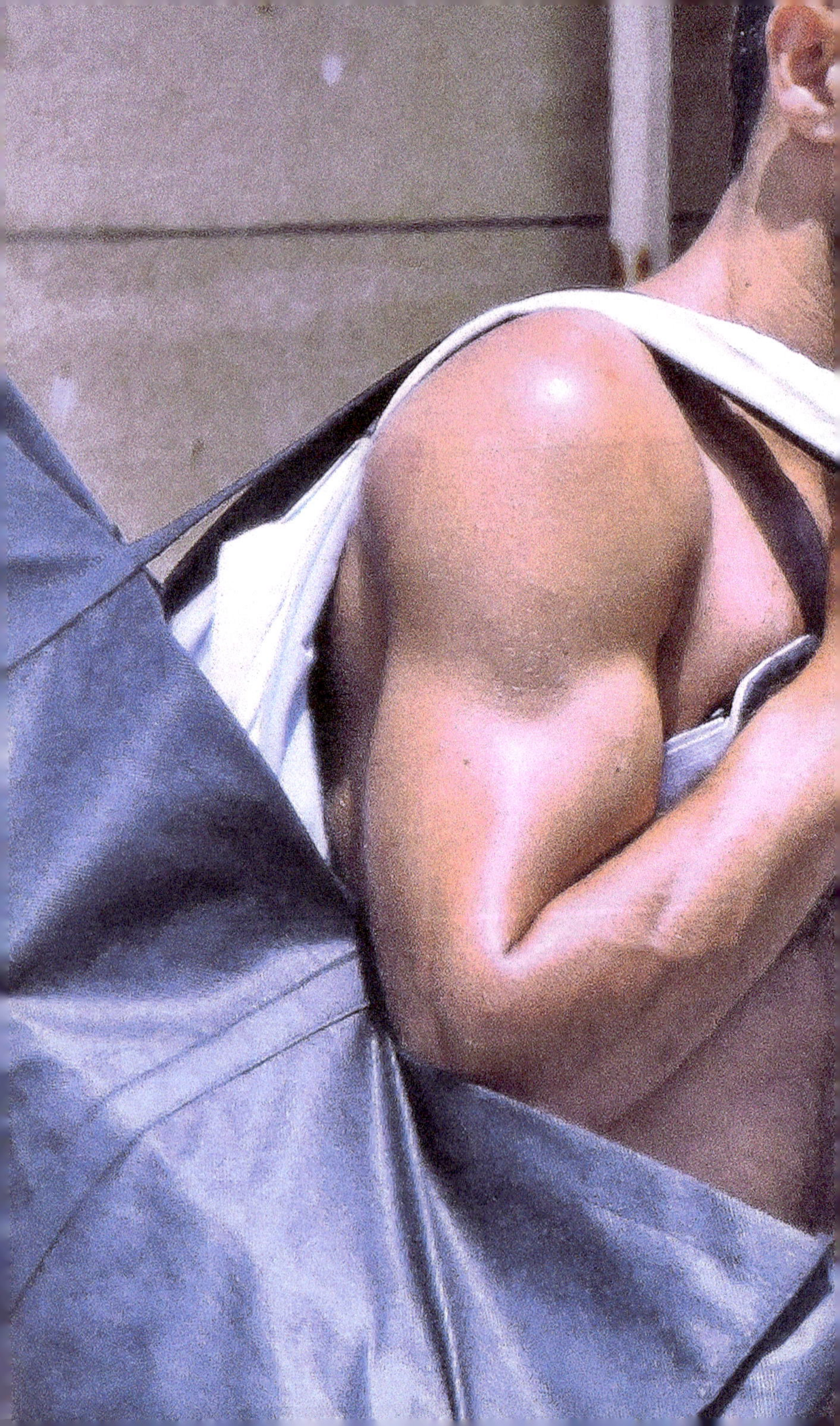

אל

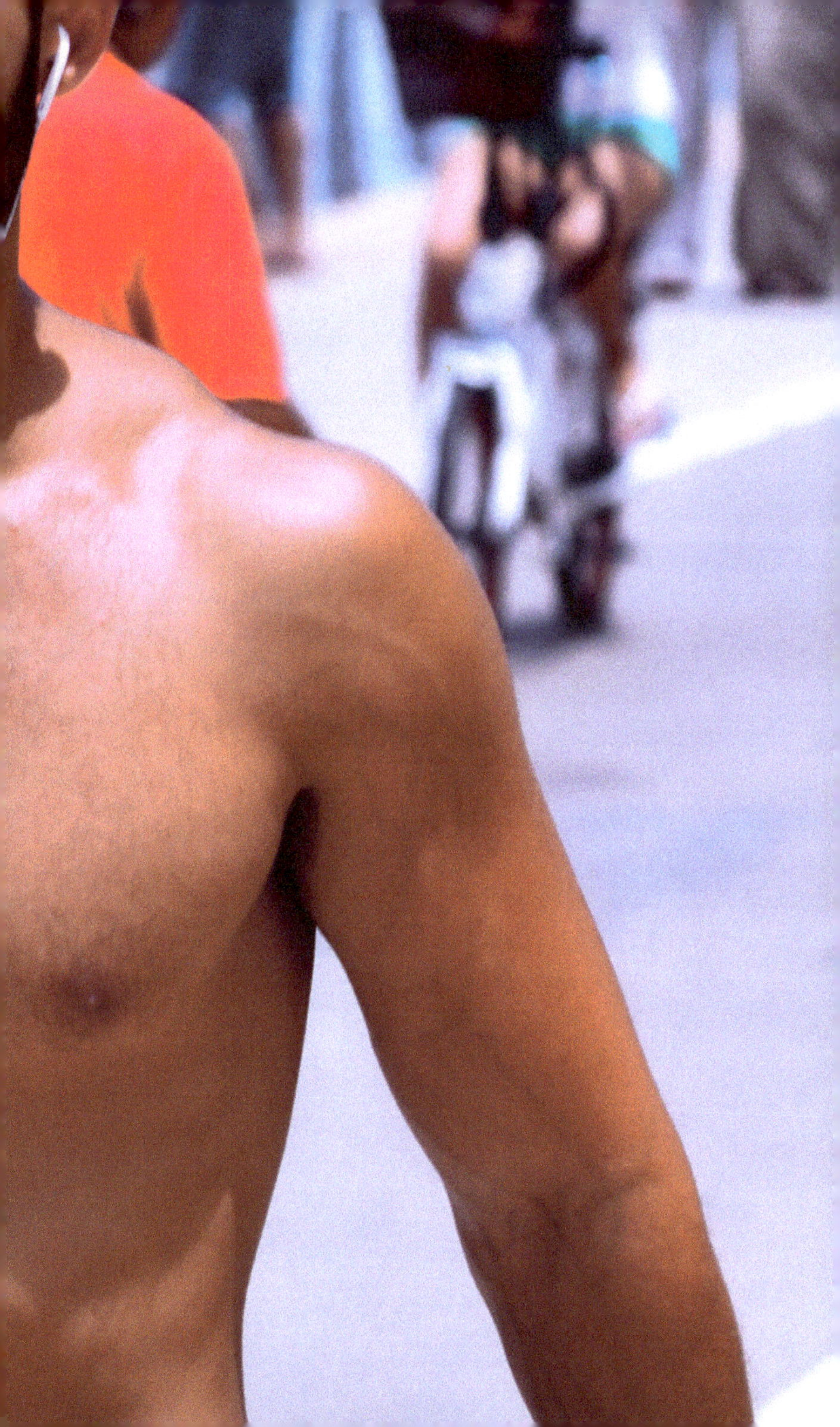

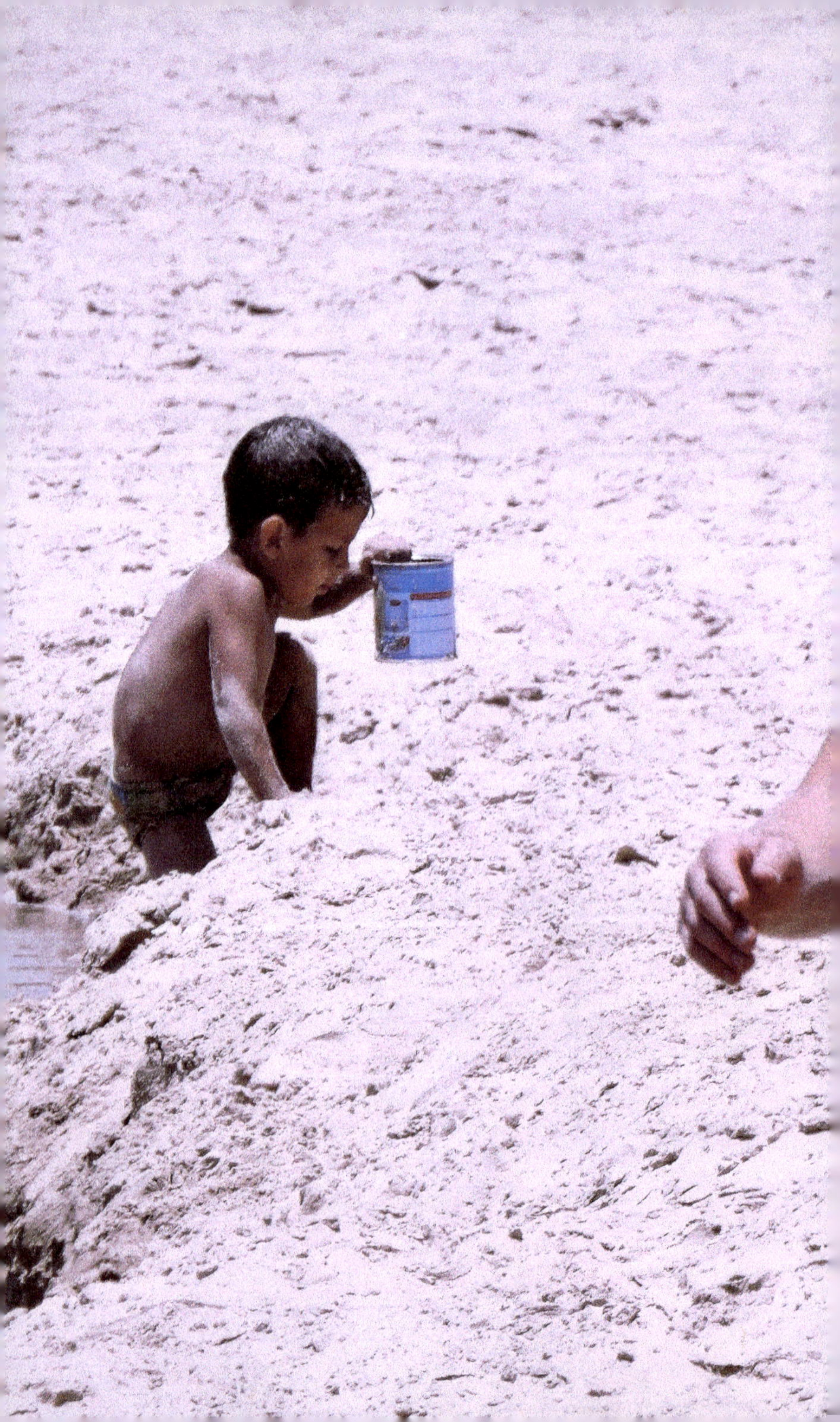

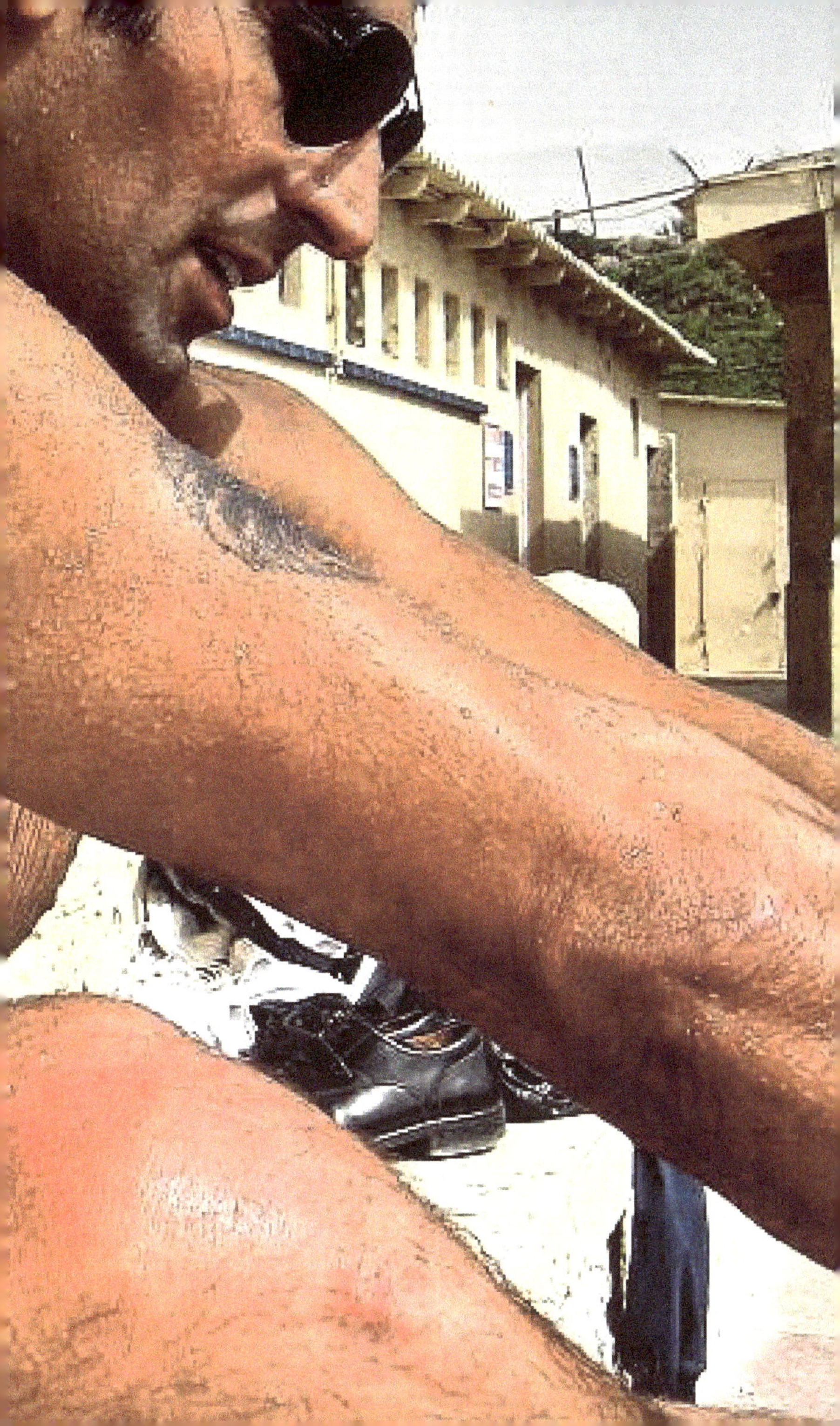

CPSIA information can be obtained
at www.ICGtesting.com
Printed in the USA
BVHW021320190619
551409BV00019B/553/P

9 780368 895630